M000306271

ALCHEMY
OF
AWARENESS

RAELENE BYRNE

Author: Raelene Byrne

ABN: 85 821 564 410

Website: www.raelenebyrne.com

Email: admin@raelenebyrne.com

Facebook: medicine for your spirit

Instagram: byrneraelene

Copyright: 2019 Raelene Bryne

Company: Medicine For Your Spirit

First Published: 2019

The moral rights of the author have been asserted.

All rights reserved. This book may not be reproduced in whole or in part, stored, posted on the Internet, or transmitted in any form, or by any means whether electronically, mechanically, by photocopying, recording, or any other means, without permission from the author and publisher of the book.

Edited by: Bermingham Books

Designed by: Bermingham Books

Typesetting: Bermingham Books

Printed and bound in Australia by: Ingram Sparks

ISBN: 978-0-6485305-1-0

CONTENTS

INTRODUCTION

CHAOS SIGNALS CHANGE and delivers us into creativity, then new choices for change in you begins.

Alchemy of awareness is an offering for transformation and transcending where you are now towards who you are becoming.

The old world utilised alchemy, a precursor of chemistry, to turn base metals into gold, so in our current times, it is about turning dense things that no longer have value or work for us, into a higher calibre of beingness, that adds value to life.

We are transcending our old selves into a more expansive higher vibration of self, moving away from survival mechanisms towards thriving and flourishing.

What was important in the past, may no longer be working for us. The 'awareness' that we can initiate the changes aligning with more of our majestic selves, listening to the call and taking new actions, is a form of alchemy, which in these current times we call evolution.

The universe is always evolving, expanding and growing, and over the last few decades human consciousness has woken up. No longer can we pretend we are something else, or be less than what we are truly here for. It feels like we were born to be the cat-alysts of change in these historical times.

There always comes a day when you wake up and realise you are living a life that is far from connected—filled with things you are not thrilled with; perhaps relationships, jobs, even where you live.

Signals for change have been sent out from deep within you. The dis-ease (your life not being at ease), the chaos, the wanting to give up, means your 'comfort zone' has just turned terribly un-comfortable—offering two options, change or stagnate.

This book is a series of topics to help you gain another insight, a different way of seeing life—perhaps helping you to connect a bit more with the eternal wisdom that you carry.

I believe with every part of my being that:

Everything we need to know we already have within, all we need do is listen, take action, and evolve towards our soul purpose.

Life can become your daily creation, filled with connection, support, awareness, peace and acceptance among many ben-efits.

Alchemy of awareness.

This book can be used as a daily inspiration, a daily change and a point of reference when unsure. Hold the book between your hands at heart level and feel what your question or interest is then open the book anywhere.

There are activities at the end of each article. Taking time to contemplate, to exercise that connection to our inner wisdom, to be with your soul, helps us to focus or receive some deep peace, answers, new insights, inspiration and the ability to make change in all areas of your life.

Taking action helps us change.

Writing things down is important. You take an energetic impulse, which we call a thought, and bring it to physic. Through the action of picking up a pen or pencil and writing something on paper, you have just brought energy into form.

Once you have things written down, you have a reference point where change begins. Remember that when we change one thing in our life, we begin a ripple effect that affects all things.

Each article will have a 'declaration' to be said once a day. Declarations are a command to the universe. You come from a level of authority within yourself to deliver that declaration. The energy response is life changing when you access this properly. You have a bigger force that collaborates with you. There is certainty activated within when we declare our intention or desire out loud.

This is the necessary set up for offering a declaration:

- You MUST stand, or sit, straight up so your back is aligned

- Close your eyes

- Visualise that you are standing in front of an army of soldiers from horizon to horizon

- They are looking at you, waiting for their next order or command

- You then state internally...the next thing I say WILL be obeyed...(feel what happens in your body when you state this)

- Then with a breath, state out loud the declaration at the end of the verse (as per the declaration in the section you have opened the book at)

- Stay in that space for a couple of breaths

- Open your eyes

- Go about your day

You have set up an energetic call to action, a collaboration with a higher energy source.

Be aware of how you feel.

State the declaration once a day, each day, for a week. This offers you the intention that connecting to your soul is a simple process of listening to your own soul; it knows the way!

ENOUGH...

AT SOME POINT our wellness, health and vitality will be interrupted by an illness like a virus.

It often takes something like this for us to stop, take stock of where we're at, and connect back with what our bodies need. To pause what we're doing, and take a rest—eat better, sleep, take baths, get some fresh air and sunshine, sometimes we need to cocoon ourselves, and take more vitamins.

We become proactive while the virus runs its course. We take care of ourselves, we engage in the 'healing' process. We allow the virus its right of passage, and we know it is NOT really us; it is an invader, a gift reminding us how we can treat ourselves better.

We know that the virus has a short life span. It can knock us over, we can feel bloody awful, and we will call it, 'I am unwell, so I am taking a few days off to deal with it'.

When any of us suffer from 'not enough', whether it's not good enough, not enough time, not knowing enough, not savvy enough, not fit enough, not thin enough, not enough money, not enough work, not enough options, blah blah blah, we should recognise these moments as a 'virus' and become proactive in dealing with it too!

We know the 'not enough' that knocks our confidence around is not true—it is like a belief lying dormant, that arises when we are disappointed, lethargic, comparing ourselves, feeling like we aren't doing anything. When we've lost direction and purpose, we can't imagine any new goals, we feel stuck or in the place of experiencing the mundane. We can't allow the 'not enough' virus to take over.

When we are weak, our immune system is open to virus and bacteria, so our body is taken over by feeling ill. Our emotional and mental states, when weakened by battling old beliefs, disappointments or rejections, will succumb to 'not enough' to play out the story. This is your opportunity to recognise that this is NOT who you are—it is only a belief or pattern that has been entrenched from earlier in life, or through the ancestry of our families.

Treating your moments of 'not enough' as you would a virus by becoming proactive, taking care of yourself and remembering who you are will help you find things that will uplift.

Normally we feel like absolute crap with a virus, it's the same thing when 'not enough' enters our awareness, but we can treat it lovingly, kindly, understanding it is showing us a deeper obstacle that is NOT really who we are—it is just an experience, a reset or a rite of passage to align with and become who we are.

Oprah Winfrey once said that nearly every one of the famous guests interviewed on her show always asked at the end, 'How was that? Was that ok?' There is something deeply ingrained in the humanness of us all, seeking perfection, to be approved of, yet, all we need at soul level is to accept ourselves, imperfect, yet unique.

As we work on strengthening our immune system to deal with any virus, maybe we can find a way to work on our 'not enough-ness'.

The following declaration can be a great boost, like taking a dose of vitamin B.

DECLARATION

Today, I am enough.
Always have been, always will be!

ACTIVITY

Intention:

To keep your head and heart from sinking into the depths of feeling *blah* when the 'not enough' rises. This is YOU choosing to be actively engaged by taking a new response to what you're feeling.

Action:

- Create a list of up to 10 things you love to do, make sure they fill you, make you smile, open you up to a higher vibe

- Thank it, then go do something you LOVE from that list
- Each morning look into the mirror after cleaning your teeth and speak your declaration out loud then smile at your enough-ness self

Have a cracker of a day!

Transitioning...

TRANSITIONING FROM ONE state of being into a new phase requires great willingness, fuelled with unwavering trust to allow things to unfold as they are meant to.

As unpredictable as life can be, we still go through the growth process of awareness, decision, action, outcomes and then transition—that grey area most of us are uncomfortable with and do our best to delay or avoid.

Transitioning between achieving and starting something else is also an expression of the process. It is a time to pause, to recalibrate and reset, a time to integrate all that you have previously worked towards so your whole personal vibration can align with that latest outcome. You are allowing a new aspect of you to emerge, changing personal and energetic dynamics.

It isn't easy when all we have been conditioned to do is to set a goal, achieve, set another goal, achieve. We celebrate briefly, yet our minds are already setting, plotting and scheming the next project, goal or outcome.

Transitions bring up loads of uncertainty about where we are going, which can throw us off our purpose or pathway as we feel

9

like we spiral into a void of nothingness. Our motivation seems lost, our sense of value is questioned, and then the scratching around trying to find something to fill that weird void begins.

The ability to allow the 'nothingness' is a great choice. It is the 'afterglow' of achieving—the space between breaths, the opening to other possibilities from a new vibrational awareness in self, the resting in the discovery of a new aspect of self. From nothing, all of life was created. This is a profound time to BE and allow what is next to formulate and deliver to you in the right time.

Imagine you are climbing a set of stairs and you come to the landing before the next set of steps. That landing is the integration point where you can 'catch your breath', before you move to the next sequence of stairs.

Transitions in life are like landing points, places to reset, recalibrate, to allow all of you to integrate before you move on again.

These become our new reference points. If we fall from the steps we are climbing, we will only go back to the last reset point, the last landing. Here we can gather ourselves, regroup and re-start from that point, not from the beginning.

In the transition time, enjoy the space, do things that nourish you knowing that your whole self is aligning to the new information, experience or expansion.

Everything in life is in transition, always shifting, growing, releasing, rebuilding or evolving. Our humanness becomes impatient, so if this occurs, do something new, open your mind to a different experience, while in the transition time. The transitioning phase does come to an end—we can't force it to be any faster than it needs to be. We need to surrender into the opportunity to renew our vision of self.

DECLARATION

Today, I align with the wisdom of my soul
as I move through a purposeful transition.
I trust this process with all that I am.

ACTIVITY

Intention:

When a caterpillar goes into its cocoon to transition into a butterfly, we often think about the romantic nature of the transformation. Yet within that chrysalis, acts of destruction and violence occur as one body disintegrates to create something that emerges with elegance, grace and lightness.

Transitions can be tough, so creating space to allow things to occur is a gift of trust to yourself.

Action:

When you are transitioning:
- Know how you want to feel, no matter what is occurring in your life or the world outside of you, i.e. secure, free, valued, safe, supported, grateful
- Clarify your thoughts and feelings—journal
- Take some walks in nature
- Meditate
- Have some healing treatments
- Stay connected and grounded to you
- Be aware of how you think and lift thoughts to a higher calibre

Remember you are NOT waiting for things to happen, you are in process, and things will be revealed at the most aligned moment.

CHOOSING...

CHOOSE SOME GENTLENESS for yourself and follow through on it.

There are so many energetic peaks and troughs happening for all of us. We feel really energised one day like we can conquer *all* things, then two days later it is all we can do to drag ourselves to the loo!

Our human density is feeling the challenge of our energetic higher nervous system and light body in full throttle.

If you have been feeling exhausted, not so much physically incapable, but a deeper sense of tiredness, then be gentle with you. The night time internal electrical buzzing, the ear ringing, the solar plexus area being hit with higher energy, the need to sleep, the intensity of loud noise or being intolerant of noisy spaces are all part of this.

Every now and again, I feel the 'harshness' of life cloaking me, and the weight of it can be unbearable. I have taken a number of weeks off from daily social media, from daily writing, from daily 'have to do this today' lists, and have surrendered into being with all of me. Fully present, gentle, attentive and listening to the wisdom running within me.

Watching the media crucify a mother for being protective, seeing innocent people being victimised, witnessing families losing their homes to indiscriminate bombing, can disrupt, disturb, and cut us to the core of decency, and we feel we have had enough.

The time is now! Gentleness needs to be the united call to action. It starts in our everyday life, our thoughts, actions, words and feelings.

If you want to feel better, then choose what you CAN do. We cannot change some of the events happening, we cannot influence the governments or the media with our beliefs about parenting, education, wellness, wholeness, justice, environment, however, we can take action in our 'supposedly' small daily lives.

Light a candle for peace, or awareness, or clarity and devote it towards the world or an event that is troubling your heart and soul. Say a prayer, set an intention then repeat it every day. These small, gentle actions preserve your heart, keep your mind focused on what is possible and keep your soul soft.

To some, this may seem woo-woo, but for me, practicing this daily has helped with my focus, knowing that my thoughts, actions, words and feelings are being sent into the bigger picture from an open heart and with a gentleness for all.

If we keep reacting to the bigger circus of misinformation, one-sided stories, incomplete coverage, the manipulation of our own lives, then the machine has you, you are distracted from what you want to see, be and live.

Being gentle with self is part of this call to action. Take the time to hold that peace, calm, clarity and awareness as an offering to the energy field. It will have a greater effect than bitching, whinging and complaining about how bad things are. Misery begets misery...there is NO gentle hope in that.

How do you want to feel when you are speaking or interacting with others...hopeful or helpless?

Gentleness in self, the choice to let things go, let things be, let life be what you want, without the daily struggle to get things done.

Yes, I know this sounds like nothing would ever be accomplished...you know what, some days you get nothing done, and that is how it has to be. It really is ok to stop, say, 'Enough for now, I need space to recharge, reset, revitalise, recalibrate'. Then other days you get more done than you could possibly imagine.

Gentleness requires an acceptance—it is part of our inner nature, it makes us take a breath, reset, find a way to be supported or supportive. What we must be mindful of is the intense work happening in our energy field, our higher self. Our physicality is dense and heavy; our higher self is a faster vibration. How can something high and strong land in our lives if we are pushing, struggling, striving and doing? There must be a space and place for things to align and merge. Creating that opportunity comes from gentleness.

DECLARATION

Today, I invite and I invoke the frequency and vibration of 'gentle' to move through me, and around me.

ACTIVITY

Intention:

Be kind, gentle and tender with yourself and others for the day.

Action:

- Purchase a large candle, in a colour that reminds you of gentleness (soft pink, soft blue, white) and etch (use a pen, skewer or sharp object) into the candle these words, 'Gentleness with self, peace in my world'
- Light the candle each day, say the choosing declaration
- Take a few moments to sit still, eyes closed, breathe gently, hands resting in your lap
- See the word GENTLE in your mind's eye
- Take a breath with intention of this energy activating within you to each of your energy centres
- Take three breaths at heart centre to seal this

SELF-LOVE...

I WOULD LOVE to introduce you to my best friend. She is weird, quirky, blunt and direct. She has a heart that beats for the planet. I love that about her.

We share the same passion for yoga, smudging, meditation, rituals, ceremonies, self-empowerment, truth, nature, sunshine, sacred music and information on planetary and evolutionary change. We have a few secret giggles, and we have our own language.

Time is never a problem, we can take as long as we like doing what we love, lingering over a chai, gazing into open fires, we love reading the same books, and eye roll at the same things.

Our walks on the beach are filled with rich, deep inspirations, messages and aha moments. We love going to the same places, watching the same movies, rock hopping, walking up mountains, and she is the best mermaid buddy ever. How did I end up with such a great friendship?

I became that person. My best buddy in life is me.

Friendships and relationships come and go in life; that is the nature of the human beast. However, you are with you all the time, you are the one constant in your life. Why not be best buddies with you?

Over the years, time on my own has become a precious joy-filled experience. I do what I love. I do not have to compromise, hurry up or accommodate others when I am with my best buddy—me.

Now don't take this the wrong way, I have some heart and soul friends who I would slay a million bulls for, would be at their side in a heartbeat and I LOVE my time with them. My life is so full because of their input, love, conversations, and shared moments.

Learning to be with yourself is a challenge for many of us, as we are so used to being entertained by external things, constantly looking for the next thing to do, wanting to fill any 'void' time with something, anything, so you have a focus point to take you away from you.

What is it that we are so frightened of in ourselves that we will do anything to avoid listening, observing, even owning? Responsibility to show up each day as you—is up to you. Self-acceptance is the beginning, the end, and everything in between in order to feel comfortable and aligned with you as you are at any moment. If you can't accept you, then don't expect others to fill that emptiness, that ache, that need...it is impossible!

Being annoyed with others, walking away from friendships, getting pinged off with other people's attitudes and actions is telling you something. Are you willing to look at it in yourself? You know I get annoyed with me at times, and I have to detach from life to face whatever is up for me, and to be honest, it is always an old pattern or thought process wanting to be let go of, otherwise, I am blocking knowing more of me. I could avoid it, and be actively engaged in being busy, but the seed of discomfort, the message of the inner world NEVER goes away until you step up or show up.

What we all have to remember is that each of us *IS* the common denominator in our life. We need to buddy up with our self, love it, nurture, have fun, be grateful, develop the dialogue, have trust, be aware, show up, and move into gentle acceptance every moment of every day, understanding we are doing the best we can.

Make yourself your best buddy and share that joy with life.

DECLARATION

Today, I gratefully and graciously honour
my ease-filled friendship with my true self.

ACTIVITY

Intention:

Reconnecting with your true self is liberating; being your best buddy is a lifelong gift.

Action:

- Take your best buddy (you) on an outing—to the movies, for dinner, coffee, juice or a wonderful adventure in nature
- Be with yourself
- Feel all the energy within as things arise
- Write a buddy to buddy letter to yourself and let all the goodness flow into the words
- Create a sacred journal just for you
- Celebrate your life as you would a friend who has had a win, success, shift, good news
- At day's start, say to yourself, 'Hey buddy, let's create a fabulous day and make it amazing.'
- At day's end, thank your buddy for a great day and say, 'Let's do even better tomorrow.'
- Ask your buddy, 'What can I do for you today?'

Treasure those moments.

TRUST...

TRUST, TRUST, TRUST in you.

As we evolve faster and gain more clarity, release the things we know are not for us, align with the life we are creating, our only real tool to walk with is trust in self.

We arrived as babies with a level of trust that all our needs would be taken care of. As we develop and grow, we take on the beliefs of life and families, losing the ability to fully trust, or to action it. Approval and acceptance from others become our number one motivation, as it keeps us safe, seemingly connected, while conforming to another's idea of who we should be. We lose the trust in self—it is chipped away, it atrophies like a muscle that is paralysed and unable to move.

Much of the lack of trust we have in self, or others, also stems from the times in life when our intuition, inner world, higher self, guide, whatever you want to call it, was telling us something and in those moments, we chose to ignore, or not to action, then later we 'suffered'.

How many times has each of us stated...'I just 'knew'—but did not take action'? That is not honouring or respect of self-trust, that is not staying true to your soul's journey. We will experience many events that bring us back to that point of 'I just knew', until one day we decide we can ONLY trust our self then you will take action.

These current times—where energy is heightened, more people are becoming aware, waking up, realising they have choices, understanding they have a right to live their own life, their own way, which requires the trust muscle to be brought back to life.

Sometimes we call it intuition, other times it is a 'knowing', and in everyday experiences, we will say, I must trust myself.

What kills developing trust or the reawakening of it, is the cloud of self-judgement, the abyss of self-doubt, the habitual way we second-guess ourselves.

Holding these things in place is the deep need for acceptance, and not wanting to be wrong. We are subconsciously terrified that if we do anything that takes us out of the pack, where we stand as an individual, we will be susceptible to attack.

Let's reclaim out birth-rights, the first being trust in self.

The steps towards finding a rich and individualised understanding of love, of living with trust, start with you. Treat yourself kindly, always. Self-trust requires you to take action and care of your needs, your safety. It means refusing to give up on you. You need to exercise kindness, and not be driven by perfection. Be aware of your thoughts, feelings, actions and how you express yourself. Stay true and aligned to your own principles, ethical codes and standards, while realising they are evolving, so self-enquiry, reflection and contemplation are required daily.

Remember:

- Care for yourself first
- Pursue what you want without limiting others
- Exercise mindfulness

Our soul wrote the life plan we are living long before we arrived. Yes, we have free will to choose various things, but the big lessons, the big wake up calls, the slap over the head reminders are already in place, as these keep bringing us back to what we are here for.

We can only walk with trust in self. We can only make decisions when we know ourselves and follow the actions with a sense of committed trust. Nothing is locked in, we can change our decisions, minds directions at any time; we are not shackled to a particular life. That was the old world; that is not real for us now.

DECLARATION

Today, I trust in my soul's journey,
I am willing to do what is required.
I walk in faith and trust with every step.

ACTIVITY

Intention:

Develop trust in yourself.

Action:

- Start your day with a deep clearing breath
- Breathe to your heart space and say, 'I invite and invoke the frequency and vibration of trust to activate within me'
- Take a breath with awareness at your feet and say, 'I trust my walk in life'
- Take a breath with awareness at your base chakra and say, 'I trust in my ability to create safety and security in life'
- Take a breath with awareness at your sacral chakra and say, 'I trust my feelings and take action'
- Take a breath with awareness at your solar plexus chakra and say, 'I trust my own power'
- Take a breath with awareness at your throat chakra and say, 'I trust my voice to communicate clearly'
- Take a breath with awareness at 3rd eye chakra and say, 'I trust my intuition and act on it'
- Take a breath with awareness at your crown chakra and say, 'I trust my connection to my higher wisdom and listen'
- Take a breath with awareness at your heart chakra and say, 'I trust in me completely'

24

- Take a full breath with the awareness that your whole body is expanding, then offer your energy field the declaration and say, 'Today, I trust in my soul's journey, I am willing to do what is required.'

TRIGGERS...

TRIGGERS ARE GREAT keys to open doors for personal growth and expansiveness when you are willing to go beneath the surface. Ideally, most of us would love to go through life without any angst, to be in a state of flowing and on purpose, living from a deep place of compassion, never getting annoyed or pinged off. What a world that would be! The reality is we all have triggers, we all have those things hiding beneath the surface, needing to be brought into the light of our awareness, or sometimes they explode around us, creating chaos, which means we waste a lot of energy in recovery.

Those moments offer us a choice, you can stubbornly stay with what is your belief and keep having the same thing ping you off over and over, or you can look at it, contemplate, ask the questions of your inner world, soften and open.

Triggers are great keys that can open doors towards more self-value, love, respect and self-knowledge.

Nothing is set in stone! Well, the Ten Commandments apparently were, yet everything is open to interpretation, via the winding laneways of our perceptions. Most of our perceptions are not even formed by us, they have been absorbed, adopted, installed as we grow, and we live with them for years, finding ourselves being 'triggered' with resistance, getting annoyed, wanting to prove our point, having to be right, when something isn't what we think it could be.

Triggers really do tell a lot about a person and what lies just beneath the surface. So, every time you feel triggered, take a breath and look at what it really is showing you, perhaps a place of resistance, a shutdown, a guardedness that blocks the opening into something more, something new, something more aligned with where and who you are in life right now. It's time to acknowledge and shift those things that are disempowering you.

One of the biggest triggers is 'expectations', followed by judgement! Triggers can be set off like fireworks as our perceptions and judgements rise to the event, occasion or situation.

When we evolve, or journey through change, others who have yet to awaken will trigger us. For example, if you have worked hard to become more empowered in your life, and you see someone you know being walked over, or giving their power away to something else, you will be irritated, inflamed or annoyed. Your perceptions will trigger the reactions through judging others for their 'lack of awareness', especially after you have been through it, transformed and evolved.

How dare any of us judge others for where they are at in life, how they are evolving, or how they are doing their own soul journey. Let's accept that we each have individualised soul paths and journeys of awakening.

Everything has a purpose. Even triggers step out of judgement, out of rescue, out of projection, into acceptance, allowing and gratitude. Sometimes a trigger is the wake-up call we need to reset or review something within our own life.

Triggers show us where judgement lives.

DECLARATION

Today, I graciously observe the energy that arises when I am triggered and courageously choose to respond with gratitude.

ACTIVITY

Intention:

Identify your triggers and work on detaching from them. Remember this is your life and you get to choose and create how you want it to unfold—triggers and all!

Develop a relationship with acceptance of self and others. Not from a getting walked over or taken advantage of, instead, from the knowing that your perceptions are different from others. Not right or wrong, just different due to life experiences and where you are you in the evolutionary process.

Action:

- Make space— stop whatever you are doing and walk away, change your environment in order to have some time to process through it

- Breathe

- Meditate

- Journal under the questions, 'How can I diffuse the energy around my triggers? Where does this emotional trigger exist within me?'

- Thank your triggers as they are showing you where more letting go needs to happen

Rest into
Be-you-is-ness...

ARE YOU IN business or are you in be-you-is-ness? There is a big shift in the world of business. More and more people are starting their own home business, creating jobs and hopefully security for themselves. The problems arise when we start living from the lack, fear, the old ways of striving to 'do, do, do' in order to be successful. We have heard the mantra, 'Do what you love and love what you do!' It sounds divine and so in flow, however not all have the capabilities or the support to enter into that realm in this moment. It can be a journey to get there.

The first step is to know you, and then to know what you love to do. Then taking the time to find ways to bring what you love to do into a way to support your lifestyle. It sometimes is a leap; it sometimes takes a few years.

The directive, or course of action, is to know what you want to offer, what you love doing as your service and how you want to feel.

Lifestyles are undergoing huge re-assessments. The era of big houses, big mortgages, big overheads, big jobs with long working hours is crumbling. There is more discontent in doing the 9-5. Those who are striving for the big end of success will commit and play in that arena. Doing everything they possibly can for the life they think they want...the status that comes with great achievements. There is absolutely nothing wrong with that. There are people born to do just that, but not everyone is born to do that!

And therein lies the seeds of discontent, struggle, the whole 'fake it till you make it' syndrome. People are burning out, getting sick, stress levels and stress leave are high, relationships are under pressure as the want to have and need to live are stretching each other in opposing directions.

So, let's all stop, draw a breath, take a few moments to re-assess:

- What does your life mean to you
- Where are your values placed
- Does your family or partner have you present, or is that something you keep telling yourself will happen once you achieve this next step, level, upgrade promotion

We are so addicted to the busy in business? What would it require for people to start prioritising their own be-you-is-ness?

Find what makes your heart and soul sing, dance, be light filled and fuelled with joyful passion. You can still work your normal job, but find a way to firstly be grateful and secondly to open a creating space for you to be you. Make that your new business (be-you-is-ness); the way forward this millennia.

For those in small business, home business—you are what people want. What you offer and do, is your business card, what people want is your energy/frequency. Make that yours, be-you-is-ness. It will be unique, different and sought after. Copying others, following another person's perceptions takes you away from you, find what you love, and do that. You will be surprised how that be-you-is-ness will grow.

One of the big concepts of business in the next few years is to take rest! Of self-nurture, not so new, but definitely needing to be a bigger focus in life. The business of you in life is the BE-YOU-IS-NESS you need to take care of on all levels.

As we step out of the old world and move towards the new energy, the old belief of being busy, staying busy, making sure your time was filled with being productive is failing to deliver the big promises of success. Instead we are seeing the rise of sickness, stress, adrenal fatigue and exhaustion.

We can feel guilty if we take a nap; take some time out to rest. What normally happens is we push, play the 'busy, busy' card until we get sick, feel unwell or become exhausted, which enforces rest, but it is really a time of recuperation.

Weekends gift us the perfect time to put our feet up, chill out, fill our own energy reserves, allow our body to reset. Don't wait until you are dragging yourself around to finally stop.

Self-care, or nurture, is a responsibility that we all are required to activate.

This action fills our sense of self-value, because we are saying I care enough about myself to make sure I am feeling good, and this opens us to more self-belief.

One of the best forms of self-care is rest...plain and simple. Especially now as we move towards this new human in a new energy, our physical bodies are recalibrating and realigning to a higher state of being. We are becoming more light-filled.

Think back to the start of the 20th century. People lived in houses with small windows, heavy drapes, heavy furniture, and they ate heavy foods. Things were darker in life. People worked, yet there were less distractions and more time for families to be together, communities to gather as lives and stories were shared. There was no work on weekends, so people made an effort to visit, go on outings, utilise their time to catch up on life and rest.

As we have evolved over the last 100 years, our homes have become spacious, more windows allow more light in, we eat lighter foods, yet we are doing more, are distracted more, stuck in front of digital devices, on the treadmill of doing. We work on weekends and into the night with no boundaries, no off button. No wonder we are exhausted, depleted and weary.

It is time to reassess and reframe priorities about work, play and rest. Rest isn't just about sleep it is a recovery and rejuvenating time.

Create a rest ritual on weekends, where you can swing in a hammock, read on a day bed, where time is not your master. Gift you a regular space to take rest. Go for a walk in the bush, visit a waterfall, climb a mountain, take a bike ride, wander in nature, breathe in the rejuvenating energy to restore, reset and rejuvenate. Make your weekends a time for real R&R. You will feel lighter, brighter, grounded, balanced and more appreciative of the efforts you give in the creation of everyday living.

DECLARATION

Today I give permission to nurture myself.
I embrace spaciousness to rejuvenate, renew and
recalibrate on all levels. I do without 'doing' and
everything gets done.

ACTIVITY

Intention:

To nurture yourself and take time to be without agenda.

Action:

- Rest
- Play
- Picnic

- Have a power nap
- Lay down and place some crystals on you
- Lay under a tree and gaze at the flow of life amongst the branches, wonder at life
- Listen to the sounds of nature
- Write about the following in a journal:
  - List three reasons why doing what you LOVE will change your life
  - List three reasons why you are staying where you are and how that is holding you back from your true pathway
  - What would you require to transition towards living a life doing what you love?
  - What support do you need?
  - Which mentors can you enlist to help you?
  - What time do you need?
  - How can you develop more trust in yourself and your abilities?
  - How can you begin to belief in yourself?
  - Do you feel you deserve to live a life where you can do what you love and feel fulfilled?

STRENGTH...

WITH ALL THE frequency, energy and vibrational shifting that influences us, we are required to tune to our own inner signal so what we broadcast into life is crystal clear. As our personal vibration shifts, daily attunements are required in order to receive information clearly and to 'broadcast' ourselves into the world in the most aligned and clear way we can.

Sometimes being TOUGH is required.

Each day we wake up, something's different in us. What we experienced on all levels the day before has been integrated into every aspect of our being, the mental, emotional, physical and spiritual. Our responsibility is to be aware and keep aligning, tuning in and tuning up, listening and looking for the interference so we can come back to the correct 'station'. Sometimes we can't quite find the right bandwidth or frequency, so we need to ask for help.

Working with people as a spiritual/soul mentor is extremely humbling and infinitely rewarding. I really do LOVE with all of my heart and soul what I offer as a mentor, retreat facilitator, meditation teacher, event creator, educator, 5th dimension intuitive visionary and writer.

I was recently thanked profusely, and told (in a backhanded sort of way) that I was tough, and the session was confronting. Facing our own crappy stories that keep us suffering, or even repeating scenarios and arriving at the same outcomes is not aligning anymore. It is getting harder and harder to hold that old paradigm, any victimhood we are still attached to or living is not appealing, it can be a repellent to relationships, friendships and general life.

Suffering is reliving the pain, the angst and keeping that energy alive, while we drop into the less than, poor me, look how bad life is treating me. Pain is what we feel in the moment and we participate in the healing of that on all levels by choosing to be proactive.

Sometimes it is a process of time, sometimes it is a process of letting go, sometimes it is a process of choosing another way of being.

The frequency in us all is shifting and can be like sound on a radio that is just off its bandwidth and doesn't sound clear—we must tune into our own station, tiny adjustments in order to have a crystal-clear reception.

There are times to be empathic and gentle; there are times to call it as it is. If we are ready to grow beyond, break out of something that depletes us, strip away the chaos of confusion, feeling lost, even acknowledging you have no idea what your purpose is,

I need to ask...is there really time to muck about holding hands, being patted on the back with a soothing, 'Oh you poor thing?'

Allowing others to stay in their stories can end up as enabling, which becomes a 'trigger', and eventually repels people. Holding space while a person is healing, shifting, aligning, upgrading is an empowerment process; all we need do is support them.

What people perceive as tough is the truth. When another person can call you on it, there is no place to hide. You either face it and deal with it or run away and pretend you didn't hear it or become aware of it...see how that works, as it will catch you eventually.

In these chaotic times, we can go easy, which can feel time consuming, or we can go hard with a strength that rises from our soul, as it knows what is the best way to progress. So, tune in.

When we remember that we have it all within, that we can connect to that. Have faith, belief, and trust in our own creative process in life, we are away, free, empowered, liberated and alive.

DECLARATION

I choose to be aware of who I am becoming.
I choose to release old stories and suffering.

ACTIVITY

Intention:

When the old painful stories arise imagine that you are reading a history book. You can read the information and experiences, but you are not emotionally attached, just turn the pages. The past is your history, not your now or where you are going.

Action:

Take a few minutes and do the following exercise to help you develop your inner strength:

- Close your eyes
- Place your hand on your heart
- Breathe and connect to that space
- Repeat with each inhalation, 'I choose to be aware of who I am becoming'
- Repeat with each exhalation, 'I choose to release old stories and suffering'

RESISTANCE...

THE MORE YOU show up to be who you truly are, the more you lift your personal frequency, the more you align with your soul's purpose, the more likely it is you will be judged, attacked, criticised and discredited. How exciting! People take notice!

To realise in those times of challenge that you can respond from your consciousness, instead of reactivity and old knee-jerk actions, is a knowing of awareness and responsibility of self.

How exciting that you can witness your childhood wounding of not being enough, or being inadequate; remembering how the fear of rejection from the tribe squashed you into the box of normal for the ultimate goal of being accepted. Even the memories of how the education system silently stole your individuality, that unique imprint that you are, to be offered the reward of badges of conformity, celebrating the conditioning of uniformity of little ones, all doing and thinking the same, while downplaying, even punishing, those who shine in their own self.

No wonder when we get challenged we can go into old patterns of defensiveness, lash out, want to prove ourselves right, or we go into the silence of diminishing ourselves, just to be accepted. The inner words say, 'Please love me, please accept me, please let me be a part of your group. I will do what you do, I will play a role that fits your normal, just see me as one of you'.

Recently I was listening to a Facebook live show with a woman I admire. The 'trolls' (those in fear), were out in full force as she delivered her wisdom and guidance to the many who were on the call to listen. I loved her way of dealing with those sending very inappropriate and hateful messages; it was like watching Wonder Woman deflect all the comments with her wristbands, while holding a deep and meaningful conversation with the group…as the comments would appear, she would block them, very elegantly and powerfully.

There is more and more of this behaviour happening as more of us start to shift into higher consciousness, awareness, taking responsibility for life, owning our stuff and moving towards our life of purpose, a soul calling and most of all living how we want to.

Do not forget, all the inner work, healing and letting go you have done to be in this space of more the empowered you. As many have not even had a connection to themselves, and are still living in a subconscious way. There is nothing wrong with that, we all wake up and get moving at different times in life. Remember, you are living your life, so do it. And allow others to live theirs in the way they are.

Resistance will show up.
How we deal with it is what is important.

Do we have to prove ourselves to others, make ourselves right so we feel ok? No...not anymore? We simply need to get on with our own life. If it feels right to us, or aligned, then live it, do it, be it. If others don't get it...too bad, so sad...that has NOTHING to do with you.

It is where they are in the moment. We can waste a lot of time and energy trying to convert others to our uniqueness, or we can simply give all that time and energy to our journey, shine it and get on with it.

When you look through history, the pioneers broke through into new territories, countries, even advances in knowledge. As they stood in the moment before committing to their calling, there would have been fear of the unknown, inadequacies of dealing with what could arise, even a sense of failure, yet the courage of needing to do something different, to follow their inspiration was the most important call to action, nothing could dissuade them, as behind their 'adventurous spirit' was the need to find places for others, to see what else is out there, to follow a call of freedom.

As pioneers in this evolutionary time, even stepping into the unknown of our own lives, we will be tested, judged, criticised and vilified. If you believe it, then you still have inner work to do; if you can let it slide off you, then you are well on your way.

DECLARATION

Today, I stand in my light, I am willing and prepared to do what is required. SHOW ME

ACTIVITY

Intention:

To discover where the resistance is within you, how you can turn the resistance into acceptance and what bridge needs to be built to take you forward.

Action:

- Close your eyes, take a few breaths with your hand on your heart
- Allow yourself to relax and drop into your heart's wisdom
- Visualise a flame in your heart, you choose the colour
- See the flame flickering, steady, strong, calm, sure
- Offer any feelings of resistance into the flame, or request that the flame bring to it resistance from places you may be unaware of
- Stay with this for a few minutes, allowing the flame to dissolve and transcend any ideas, feelings, experiences of inner resistance
- Practise regularly

Awakening...

WHEN WE FINALLY awaken and connect to our deeper nature, we realise the best teacher exists within. Recently I was asked, 'Who is your teacher?' My response, without any thought, was…I am. The person who asked looked slightly surprised, expecting some guru's name to be offered. I wasn't being a smart arse, it was a truth delivered straight from my inner world, or from soul.

Now I don't mean to sound like a know-it-all. It has taken me many years to finally understand the first 'real words' a teacher spoke to me when my awakening process began.

Everything you need to know you already have within.

The reality for each of us these days is, if we are connecting within, remembering who we are, even asking that simple question, we are going to the truth of our own soul's wisdom, we are listening to our own inner teacher.

Teachers, inspirational people, gurus, influencers are all over the planet. They share their perceptions of life, spirituality, through their own life experiences. What happens is many people listening or reading, will relate to their stories of hardship, struggle, maybe abusive childhoods or deprivation and then to see someone rise above it, transform their life, hold their destiny in their hands, inspires us to remember, to take new actions, to understand we are here for something, we can rise above our own individual hardships.

We want to know HOW. So, we turn to people of authority for answers. They are showing us their way, their experience, their knowledge…and perhaps opening us up to our own discernment of what works for us, and what doesn't.

Another person's way may not work perfectly for anyone else as it is their own experience. Teachers come in many forms apart from those we look up to. When we are present to life, we see teachers everywhere…nature, kids, interactions with others, billboards, conversations, movies and books.

Anything or anyone that initiates questions around what you are doing and why; any situations screaming for change, any feeling that something isn't right, is a teaching! How you respond to the call to action or lesson is up to you. The best teacher is your last mistake. How often do we say, 'I will learn from that'?

There are many ways to eat an apple. You can chop it, cook, it, peel it, cube it, quarter it, halve it, eat it whole, put it on kebabs, add cheese to it, stew it, grate it, puree it, make a sauce…and on it goes.

We eat an apple the way we were fed when young, see this example as a belief being gifted to us. We continue our whole life eating the apple a certain way because that is what is ingrained in our thoughts. Then one day someone offers you an apple done differently, you may reject it, as you like yours a certain way. Then finally you give it a try, and ooohhh what a different experience, you start to eat it that way in your everyday life. Then we start to experiment, trying different ways…or maybe the quest becomes to find different ways to eat the apple every day…opening you up to unlimited possibilities.

Teachers offer information to open you to a new experience, which initiates a desire to know more, to remember more, to expand, to question. We create the experiences we live through so we can apply the new information or wisdom to grow our soul and life. Then one day, as you are more confident in your own abilities to attempt different things, you decide to listen more intently to your inner knowing, the world within and follow its direction, its teachings.

So, we keep creating lessons, our higher self, soul, spiritual self, in order to change things, realise we can do something different, we can let go and we can move forward towards what we know is available for us or more aligned.

We all need inspiring people, influencers, teachers to remind us to open within, expand outwardly, to know thy own self, to live with awareness and show up each day offering that best part of self. You are your best teacher, you live and grow through all of your life experiences, as you have created and co-created them for your own learning.

We have an unlimited potential and infinite wisdom within to access.

DECLARATION

Today, I AM awakening and realigning my energy body system into my highest Soul Essence and divinity.

ACTIVITY

Intention:

Do something new and see how things change around and within you.

Action:

- Explore different books or writings on soul, spirituality, awakening

- Watch a video or shows to instil a sense of enquiry, to expand your mind

- Ask questions, don't just take everything as truth, be curious

- Book a class or workshop to learn a new skill or craft, perhaps learn an instrument or a new language

- Change some set-in routines by doing one thing differently or in a new sequence and watch how that shifts other things in life:

    o   Drive a different way to work

o   Try a new food each week

o   Cook something brand new once a week

o   Do that thing that scares you

o   Visit new places

BALANCE...

ONE OF THE new stress factors in life, adding to a long list, is the pursuit of balance in all parts of life. Huge business has been built on finding balance. Life has created such huge demands, well we have bought into the story of what makes us successful, that most people are so entrenched in doing, achieving and accomplishing while keeping their heads above water, that they have forgotten how to play, be and have fun.

When we are balanced, we seem to handle things easily, are more productive, better focused, and funnily enough happier due to less stress. There is a sense of ease, while the priorities we have in place support the life we live.

Living in these fast times of do more, achieve more, be more, tips the scales from balance to chaos. One of the first things we lose in the pursuit of achievement is time for self, which is demonstrated by less time spent on health.

The story we tell ourselves is, once I get these things done, get on top of this list of things to do, get ahead, I can look after myself.

Finding balance isn't a hard chore,
or a time-consuming exercise, it is merely choosing you
as a priority and creating space in your life
to keep you connected, in flow and steady.

Sometimes when we are under the pump, we let something go, we change our routines, maybe get up a bit earlier to have that space for self.

Earth cycles around the sun for 365 days. In that journey, there are two 'universal reset' points dedicated to balance; they are the equinoxes. These occur in autumn and spring reminding us of the equal day and night hours, light and dark. An equinox is when there is equal light and dark in a 24-hour cycle. Light doesn't rule over dark and darkness doesn't rule over light. A point of balance is part of a cycle!

Some of the cycles we experience are the 365-day yearly dance of the earth around the sun, the 28-day monthly dance of the moon around the earth, the 24-hour cycle of our planet between sunrises. When we know our personal cycle, in the bigger picture, you realise that balance is a momentary thing.

Check in a couple of times a day and ask yourself, 'Am I in or out of balance right now?' and 'What is required to bring me into a point of balance?' Often, once we attain that, we shift out of that space, just as the earth finds its reset point of balance only twice a year.

Each day we arise to a new aspect of self, something is different from the day before, yet, we are still living in the universal cycles around us—a universe in constant expansion. Being in balance all the time can be a stressful achievement. Being in flow, knowing your own cyclic nature, trusting the process of your life as you have created it, being open to what else is arriving/arising and making sure you find that new reference point of balance each day, for a brief moment, helps us with being in balance, not working at finding balance.

Bringing your energy field into balance provides the conditions for having an equal amount of giving and receiving within all things. As most of us are terrible at receiving, the remedy is simple...say thank you to compliments, say yes when someone offers to help you, ask for help if you require it.

When you are open to receive, you are gifting another person the ability to give...it brings joy to both sides.

DECLARATION

Today, I honour myself, and all that I am.
I allow effortless balance to surround my life and day.

ACTIVITY

Intention:

To feel the balance; to feel the joy.

Action:

- Go outside, place your bare feet on the ground/earth/sand/rocks
- Take a few breaths of equal duration of inhalation and exhalation
- Express gratitude
- Open your arms to the cosmos, take some breaths in and visualise you are taking that through you
- Bring the universal reset of balance into and through your body, and anchor beneath your feet
- Try rock hopping as a great way to find balance as you move
- Do some balancing yoga postures—tree pose, find that still point within to allow balance to anchor

STEADINESS...

ENGAGE IN STEADINESS as a daily activity. Being steady stems from a sense of confidence in self. Being steady is a moment where you are firm in you, grounded, focused, balanced and able to keep moving with that in mind. No matter how 'aligned' we think we are, distractions, miss-out-itis, rushing ahead and not looking where you are going can create a state of chaos, fragmentation, uncertainty, even a place of feeling lost.

We need to engage in being steady. We pause, we ground, we take a breath, we reset, we refocus and we find our balance again.

Whatever we are doing—sport, academia, working, creating, dreaming—there is a point where we require steadiness to give us a reference point. Steadiness is an important state of wellbeing. In the steady state, you find it easy to do what you commit yourself to do. There is a sense of inner calm.

When we believe in the roles we offer life as defining us, we lose that inner light, the steady flicker of divinity, ever witnessing that takes us into unchartered waters of chaos, crisis and uncertainty. We lose ability to find our way home to self as we are so preoccupied with external life.

In shamanic teachings, the medicine wheel is a place we approach to find the core within, to feel contained. We sit in this sacred circle relying on everything that is already there. We allow the wisdom of life to reveal the answers to an issue, the actions to reclaim ourselves to find our centre. It is timeless; no rush, no expectations, no rules, just you being steady within yourself.

We feel steady when there is a level of balance between our thoughts and emotions, when we can be non-reactive, more of an observer of life.

Cultivating a practise of quietness within delivers a steady heart, mind and soul; opens us to patience needed to develop steadiness not only in regards to our fears and worries, but also in the face of the reactions of others.

We cannot let the thoughts and emotions of others affect how we feel ourselves. People will praise our actions one day, and then on another day, the same people will critique the deeds that we have done. There is nothing that we can do to change this; it is the way of the world. Our steadiness needs to transcend the moods and opinions of others. Our steadiness needs to come from within.

Patience, understanding, confidence and faith are some of the qualities we gain from finding that state.

Finding that point within of being steady is not rigidity—it is an empowered state of being.

Imagine for a moment a baby taking their first steps...you watch all the muscles in their feet working to find that steadiness, that balance. Once mastered, walking is not even a conscious action, it happens.

The same applies to us, finding that point within each of us, the calm steadiness of knowing, once we master that, we have a place to reside when all else is uncertain. The external circumstances can change, yet the 'inner knowing' stays the same.

DECLARATION

Today, I confidently choose to stand
on my own two feet and take action from the
heart wisdom that speaks through me.

ACTIVITY

Intention:

To quiet yourself and feel what happens in your body.

Action:

- Close your eyes, take a breath and state, 'I invite and invoke the frequency of steadiness to activate within and around me'

- Visualise yourself sitting in a circle, or a medicine wheel in the wilderness
- Realise that you have all that you need inside this safe circle, you are the centre of this circle
- Keep your focus and attention on you being in the centre of that circle
- Breathe to relax and feel a sense of calm
- Breathe into you what you require for steadiness
- Know that the only thing changing is you, nothing outside of you has
- Sit in this space for a few breaths
- Stand up, feet balanced on the earth
- Close your eyes
- Breathe
- If are you rocking, swaying, moving, losing your footing or feeling disorientated, then practise the first activity, and try this again

INNER LIGHT...

YOU HAVE AN inner light requiring attention. Firstly, we have to recognise that we all have a powerful inner light that makes each of us unique. A tiny spark, flame or flicker of divinity existing in each of us, making us unique, unlike anything else, the universal thumbprint so to speak, like a single candle flame or a pilot light.

I love creating crystal grids, mandalas and labyrinths with candles. Each candle, though it holds its own space, has a unique position in what I am creating, combining with all the other candles to bring to life something that I could only vision or imagine. Our inner light, like the candles in my grids, is a part of creation and contributes its uniqueness to a much bigger story, a much bigger vision.

By itself, a pilot light or candle flame holds a steady constancy of the potential for you to remember you. It needs attention; more gas, juice, fuel to become something that allows it to shine fully. Connecting us to something greater; yet individualised for each of us to experience our own human journey. That inner light is important. We are required to turn it up—to deliver that potentiality of self towards the bigger picture in this life, and the family of humanity. When we juice it up, we take actions in life where we are being purposeful, have direction, filling ourselves, engaging in self-value, belief, love, taking responsibility for all of our life with a willingness to keep evolving. The result is a radiance; something palpable, tangible, something that can't be missed.

When we see people who are aligned, on fire, happy, know where they are going, or a person who has gone through a transformative shift in energy, we will remark…that person is radiant, or they are shining, glowing, even lit up.

That is the light within, the soul fire displaying itself. Every cell is lit, the energy field is expanded; there is such a force of recognition of self. Once you experience that, you will do all that you can to stay in that energy or feeling.

When we feel off, unwell, lacking in energy, on the wrong track, depleted, in blame, lack, or stuck, our pilot light is dimmed down. We need to look at how we are turning it down within the self. What habits, actions, beliefs are keeping your light dimmed? What can you offer towards the pilot light to fuel it, to turn the volume up?

You know the flicker of divinity is there…the twinkling in eyes, the burst of laughter, the tear drop that quietly slides down a cheek, the generosity of spirit to help another in need, the moment of deep connection with nature, even in the times of sacred actions. What is the best way to shine your light, to radiate your potential? You being you…simple, true and maybe not always easy, but at least you know what fires you up, what dims you down. Pay attention and take action.

There are times when we need to retreat, and it appears that our light has been dimmed...we may need to recover, recalibrate, reassess, re-balance, re-align, reconnect, within to see what adjustments are required for a brighter light to shine out so we don't have to berate ourselves. We only need to allow, maybe we are adjusting to a new fuel! Something new to help our lights shine even stronger.

DECLARATION

Today I stand in my expansive, infinite light.
I am prepared to do what is takes. Show Me!

ACTIVITY

Intention:

Look inside and see how you can help your light shine brighter.

Action:

- Stand tall. State out loud:

  This light that I am, keeps me safe

  This light that I am, knows my path

  This light that I am, guides me

  This light that I am, delivers my potential

This light that I am, is courageous

This light that I am, is bright, aligned, balanced,

This light that I am, radiates all that I am.

- Take a breath; place your hand on your heart and say,

  'The light that I am is grateful, gracious and unlimited'

RELEASING...

LETTING GO, SHEDDING the old habits, patterns, and thoughts takes time; it is a constant mindfulness call to action. When we decide to make changes in life, we can be very impatient. We have the vision, the clarity and understanding, we need to allow the old to leave and the new to arise or arrive.

So often we lose our vision of what we are heading towards due to impatience.

Imagine you have a cup of tea and you keep adding teaspoons of sugar to it, stirring each one into the liquid until dissolved. The sugar is absorbed and assimilated into the liquid. You keep adding one teaspoon at a time, making sure each one is dissolved. From the outside you don't see it, it takes a lot of sugar added to the mug, before the level of the liquid changes. The flavour is tainted, sickly, yet it can't be seen.

The same happens to us. We get lost in the creation of others. We take on other people's ideas, beliefs, patterns, expectations and directions one at a time from a young age, and they get dissolved into who we are. They become part of our belief system. More and more is added, and many of us wind up disconnected, lost, unwell and purposeless until we make a decision, or circumstances occur to create change. We start to seek a 'healthier state of being', we want to kick the 'sugar' habit.

It can't be seen from the outside, yet when you are living it, the taste of something not right is obvious. That is the moment we feel uncomfortable and realise something must change.

When we finally realise we are here to live a life of purpose, a soul calling, something unique, individualised, or even the simplicity of being happy, we need to wean ourselves off that 'sugar' so to speak. This is how we can look at the shifts happening within us right now. We are consciously and actively weaning ourselves off everything that has been dissolved into us that is not ours.

It will take time to know our own original flavour before the 'sugar' was added, to remember that correct balance.

It takes consistent actions, constant consciousness, a willingness to see it through, a commitment to know who you are and courage to say no to anything being added to you that is not yours. And like weaning yourself off anything, there will be days of challenge, difficulties, where you will be tempted to go back to the old ways. It may work for the instant gratification effect, yet your knowing will kick in as you can NEVER plead ignorance once you start the cleansing, releasing, towards the rediscovery of the real you.

DECLARATION

Today, I gratefully and graciously release, let go, dissolve and detach from all things that no longer serve me.(If you have a particular thing you are wanting to let go of, then identify that and state it out loud in declaration.)

ACTIVITY

Intention:

To consciously acknowledge what is NOT working for you anymore. By committing it to paper, by writing it out, a pathway opens for other hindrances to be seen. These actions give us a physical, emotional and mental connection to let go on all levels

The burning process is the dissolving, disintegration of what you are choosing to release.

Like in a bush fire, things are destroyed, or purified, so the renewal process is clean, clear and rapid.

Releasing anything creates a space for new things to enter out life.

Action:

- Write a releasing or letting go letter. Start the letter with, I gratefully and graciously release and let go of...
- List everything you can think of
- Finish the letter with, I set me free, I set all of this free

- Sign your name

- Across the page, from the bottom left hand corner to the top right corner, in bold letters print...AND SO IT IS

- Hold the letter to your heart. See the energy of what you wrote about streaming from your heart into the page, releasing the attached emotion

- Then burn the paper. Use a candle and a fireproof dish or if outdoors, place in a fire

EMBRACING...

SELF-ACCEPTANCE IS THE ultimate action towards embracing who we are. Self-judgement, self-criticism and diminishing ourselves are all behaviours and beliefs that keep us from being and revealing who we are. Once we accept that we are imperfectly perfect in all moments that is the fabulous gift of being unique, realising there is no other frequency like you in the whole universe, understanding that you are here for a purpose, that is solely yours to shine, radiate, contribute, make a difference—then you are on the path to embracing yourself.

Embrace those moments when you feel full (not from eating too much!), that inner sense of contentment.

***When we are embraced in fullness, a softness arises,
a generosity of spirit, a connecting to the deeper flow
in your own human experience.***

We have all had times when life has filled us with everything we need, we feel there is so much love, abundance, connection, ease, gratitude, communication, and time never seems to be involved. In reflection, you would remember that sense of softness and kindness that was ever present. It is when we energetically expand, and everything we interact with is affected by our 'fully aligned soul frequency'.

This morning I was at the beach, watching the high tide and the water felt soft; there was gentleness as each wave kissed the sand. Yet the power behind each wave was palpable, a force of movement, a delivery of energy while the water felt soft, yielding, a caress.

The oceans move, they expand at high tide, and contract at low tide; it is like watching the ocean breathe. It appears to be a constant resetting, re-aligning, a gathering and collecting of momentum. Each tide is unique; it has its own energy. How do we apply this to life?

When we feel energetically full, we expand. Everything in our world has a 'golden hue' to it, there is space, connection, contentment, knowing, we offer ourselves with a generosity of soul and a confidence that all is as it should be.

When we feel empty, not enough, not full, contracted; we can have sharp edges, prickles, barriers and resistances. We believe we HAVE to do all sorts of things to fill our life and selves; we can retreat in (contract) and start playing out the limiting beliefs, negativity and sabotage.

We believe we MUST smooth out the edges, pull out the prickles, break down the barriers, and face our resistances with an iron will of determination. We create a force to break through our crap; it is a mental force, not a gentle force. The gentle force is like the ocean waves, the trusted flow...the intent of power is there, the movement is fluid, there is a knowing and being, which confidently delivers each wave to the edge.

We can learn a lesson from this. Maybe when things are feeling angsty, depleted, contracted, chaotic, you are being asked to engage in TRUST of your own unique journey. Allow the flow to deliver you to the edge of change, find the moments that fill your soul and expand you. They may be fleeting, but they are reference points. Each reference point is a place of expansion, generosity of spirit, closer to your true self.

Sometimes everything will seem difficult, but this is when we can come from a place of self-acceptance, embrace who we are and state, 'This is just how it is right now, it won't be like this later—so I can allow, accept and embrace change as a moment by moment occurrence.'

DECLARATION

Today, I embrace and embody expansive abundance.
I am willing and prepared to do what it takes. Show me!

ACTIVITY

Intention:

To accept things in the moment and understand they won't always be like this.

Action:

- Imagine you are at the ocean/watch a video clip of ocean waves/go to the ocean if you can
- Watch the waves as they flow in and out
- Breathe with the movement of the waves…rhythmic, calm, spacious
- Stay with it for a few minutes, sensing a union with the flow
- If you have anything you wish to 'let go' of…at the edge of the water where the waves come in and out, write in the sand what you are letting go of
- Watch as the waves come in and 'take' that away for you
- Feel that flow out
- State, 'This is who I am today'

CREATING...

ASK YOURSELF THESE four questions, and you just may get some powerful insights for the steps you require in your own healing:

- When did you stop dancing?
- When did you stop singing?
- When did you stop being enchanted by stories?
- When did you stop finding comfort in the sweet territory of silence?

These are the four questions a medicine man or woman would ask you if you presented feeling disheartened, depressed, disconnected or apathetic. These questions can pinpoint when you disconnected from your soul/spirit, shut down from inner joy and peace.

A few years ago on a retreat I was facilitating in Sedona USA, we had the great honour of having Dr Steven Farmer join our group to offer his wisdom and experience as a shaman in ceremonies and rituals. When he mentioned these questions something in me responded with, 'Of course!' Like an ancient piece of the puzzle was remembered. I had to write that down.

So many of our 'current life dramas' can be alleviated by simple actions.

Dancing shakes everything up. You can lose yourself in the music, work some old stagnation out of the body; get the blood pumping, change the biochemistry in your physicality and have some very happy outcomes. Who doesn't like dancing? Those men who say they can't dance, actually can move, they just have a block around how they look when they dance, so they shut down from expressing joy in a carefree way. Come on fellas, we can all dance—even if you just sway about! And women, stop making fun of men and how they move…be grateful they are giving it a go, encourage men to move to the music.

How great is it to sing or chant? The times when your favourite song comes on and you start belting it out like you are performing in front of 50,000 people…pretending you are AC/DC, or Adele! Have you ever pulled up next to a car at lights or in traffic and the person in the car next to you is going for it, singing their heart out with all the facial expressions, hitting the high notes, without a care? I always applaud them…they are in their moment! And that makes me feel GREAT! Their energy has spilt into my world. Singing opens the throat chakra, opens your heart, gets all the cells in your body vibrating with joy. That feeling at the end, the sweet smile of 'I so rock', that lands on your face as you bow to your imaginary crowd, what a great energy you have gifted yourself.

Listening to stories…most of us were brought up on stories and nursery rhymes. Remembered the feeling of sitting close to

72

a parent/guardian as they open the book and start to read bringing all the images to life, acting things out. We had fun, we knew it was comforting and a time of focusing, but more importantly a time of connection.

The indigenous cultures have their story times around a fire; they share wisdom, experiences, and come together as a community. Children learn how to belong and what to contribute from listening to the stories; the interaction is the transmission, from people.

Silence…the world needs us all to tune inwards, to visit a place of quiet, to perhaps speak less and listen more, to enjoy life with some of the distractions turned off.

Our lives are so noisy these days. Getting out into nature, choosing to have time in silence is a healing reprieve. You must know the feeling when things are just way too loud and noisy. Imagine the feeling you have with a hangover, loud noises make you cringe…do you think your soul feels like that? If we are connected we totally feel the need for quiet time, silence. Give yourself the gift of turning all your devices off for a couple of hours, get into nature, you will feel restored.

Can you see how these four simple things could make a huge healing impact on people? On the world? Introduce them into your life and let the energy you build affect the bigger energy we are all connected to.

Years ago, I was at a festival and there was a band rocking it out. The marquee was filled with people surrounding a huge dance floor. I watched as quite a number of kids (up to about age seven) danced wildly, joyfully, moving how they wanted without a single care in the world. There were no worries of what do I look like, am I doing it right? There was just fun, letting go, while being. These kids were expressing the song, the vibration, their energy in movement. I observed many adults tapping their toes, the few odd hips swaying, yet no adult went to the floor. I started to ask the questions, 'What happens to us? What makes us stop dancing? And at what age does it seem uncool?'

I invite you to sing out, dance it up, read stories and find silence—think we have a prescription for happiness, health, vitality and joy.

Give it a go.

DECLARATION

*Today, I create my world, I am free to be me,
I am free to be me, I am free to be me.*

ACTIVITY

Intention:

Discover the road to finding the silence within.

Action:

- Put on some music you love
- Dance, move your body. It doesn't matter what it looks like…just let your body move to the groove
- Sing
- Read stories, books, tell stories to kids, listen when others tell their stories
- Meditate

PURPOSEFUL FLOW...

YOU ARE DEFINITELY not alone with all the crazy weird happening right now. The energetic tug of war between who we were and who we are becoming is really strong right now. Some people may seem to have moved through it, others are just taking the steps of awareness, and some are still not even aware of what is happening.

Let's remember our own space and soul journey and align with that. Even if you feel like you are not sure what you are meant to be doing, or creating or moving towards, or even if you feel that there seems no purpose in what you are doing...you already have awareness...that is the first step. You are already thinking about it, having those self-enquiries and inner dialogue.

If we can do something each day that fills us, keeps us moving, allows us to be filled with happiness, joy, or even something we just love doing, they are indicators of being purposeful. Not all of us are here to be high-flying successful business people, influencers, motivational speakers, New York Times best sellers, leaders in fields of importance. What we do each day when we show up consciously for ourselves, is one of the hardest, yet most courageous, things we can do as long as we do it truthfully, kindly and take actions from our inner wisdom.

We have to hold on to that as the weird crazy amps up. Attacks, personal abuse, defamation, challenges, put downs, negativity, unhealthy comments, lies, projections will keep happening as we move away from the old conditionings.

Some people just aren't ready for this new earth, the new human and some never will be. You can pull yourself back, spend loads of energy being apologetic, devalue your beliefs and choices to seemingly appease another, or you can accept that is where that person is, and you are where you are. Feel GREAT for being you and choosing to be the best aspect you can.

Offering acceptance to those who berate and belittle through their own lack of understanding sets you free to keep living what you love.

So, don't take it to heart, it is a moment of awareness. Yes, you will feel disappointed. Yes, you will feel the need to prove you are right. Yes, you will want to defend what you believe is true for you. Yes, you will want to call people out for what they are doing or saying that may hurt you or your decisions in life.

Take a big breath...let it out slowly, repeat that as many times as you like! Choosing to not react is the best first step. Understand that in most cases what people are doing or saying that have a negative impact is coming from a lack of knowledge, experience or even fear-based mentality. They are terrified of change, and the idea of others changing means their own view of life needs to be re-evaluated. There are people who just do not like, or accept change.

By holding yourself powerfully in your own light, knowing that what you are choosing for you is exactly right for you can be enough to get you over the hump. Oh and lots and lots of breathing...and in some cases, call a friend and debrief...that has saved the sanity of this soul many times!

The beauty of establishing our purpose (remember YOU are your purpose) is we can then step into the energy of flow. Allowing that wondrous knowing to keep showing us where we are meant to be, opening up deeper trust to move into who we are each day.

Flow with the universe...this is something TOTALLY different from floating along in life.

Floating is like aimlessly or subconsciously being carried by a force or current, without a clear direction, outcome or goal. It's like a cork bobbing up and down in a river; no input, no direction, just being carried. Seeing where I will end up. Sometimes we need to have space in life to float, it gifts us respite, takes us out of the plotting, planning, mind workings of strategies and schemes.

However, to be in flow is a powerful choice.

Flow means you have chosen a direction, goal, outcome, while you are showing up from a service aspect.

You are active, engaged, consciously connected. Staying in that energy of flow allows your outcome to be more, bigger, perhaps easier than your mind can imagine.

- When out of flow, we feel stressed, tense; things are hard, resistant, limited, blocked, over thinking, lacking trust, rigid, and closed. Everything will feel hard; disinterest and apathy creeps in, we feel lost, and want to give up

- When we step into flow, we feel spacious, trusting, confident, unique, attuned to signs, intuitive, open, not limited or stuck, a desire to do new things, and life feels effortless and easy

You are serving yourself, you are serving a community; you are serving something you have designed for yourself LONG before you arrived here on earth. You have surrendered to the intelligence of a greater force that moves through all of life. Flow is being in that wisdom and intelligence, which is way greater than our limited minds can understand.

At the core of who we are we know why we are here and when we finally surrender to that— and it can take lifetimes, decades, years or a clear moment in time for that to become real, remembered and embraced, without strategies—we are being in service to our soul's purpose. The universal flow of energy works with you and through you.

Look at the times in your life when things just happened, and kept happening, and you were surprised at how things aligned and were humbled by the ease or unexpected bonuses of what showed up. Those are the moments we are in flow; we are not overthinking anything, we have surrendered to what we are here to do, experience, learn and share. It is a glimpse of true co-creation and the power we have within.

Take some of the guilt and shame out of your daily self-bashings. No matter what path you are on, or which experiences you have engaged in, the moment you realise that is NOT who you really are, that it was just an experience you had to go through to bring you to the point of making decisions to change something, that is awareness, that is healing. It is your soul's song reminding you of the pathway you agreed to participate in for this life.

Flow is your agreement to keep following your path; surrendering to your highest self as it knows what is ahead, and moving with the energy of the universe, staying in the grace of your soul, no resistance, complete yet allowing with consciousness.

DECLARATION

Today I align with my soul purpose. I trust the process of my life and gratefully flow with the wisdom guiding me.

ACTIVITY

Intention:

To remind us that flow is timeless when we are involved with what we are doing and focused. The more you nurture yourself, the easier it is to achieve a level of flow.

Action 1:

- Do something that you love
- Focus on what you are doing
- For 10 minutes doodle, colour in, paint, draw, dance, do some yoga, or stretch

Action 2:

- Think about where you find flow is blocked in your life (work, family, friendships, relationship, health, wellness)
- Pick one and create a simple plan to incorporate conscious actions to move through the issues
- Close your eyes for a few minutes
- Visualise how you see yourself in a week, a month, six months, a year by staying true to your own path, your own purpose
- Write down three things you want to create in life, or become for yourself i.e. peaceful, clear, abundant, creative
- Then ask the question, 'What can I do to make that happen?'

TONE FOR THE DAY...

MORE OFTEN THAN not, when the morning alarm shrills us into wakefulness, we jump out of bed and race to achieve all the things we need to before we head off to work, take the kids to school, go to the gym, meetings and all the 'important' activities that fill our days and give us a sense of purpose.

How many of us have hard days, where we are exhausted at the end and want to flop about until we fall into bed, just to repeat the same process the next day? It has been said, 'Nothing changes if nothing changes!'

Consciously engaging in your life can be as simple as setting a tone, a vibrational intention for the day. If that is all you have time for in a morning, then make this simple awareness important.

Taking that first fully conscious breath at the start of a day and setting the 'tone' for the day you are about to engage in, create and integrate, is an empowering moment.

When we look at setting a tone for the day, we look at how we are actively choosing to harmonise, to strengthen, to flow, to create a resonance to remain in, just for a day at a time. It is the choice point of creating an overall theme for your day, breathing it in and knowing that you can draw on that throughout the day.

Choose how you want the day to be...to flow, to be seamless, to get things done with minimum fuss. Perhaps to be in a state of gratitude, or receptivity, maybe you can call on courage to move ahead, or even asking to align with the correct words if you have serious business to attend to.

There is that moment in the morning when your feet hit the floor, where you are showing up for your part of life in the day. You are committed to moving forward and only you have the power to choose how you will be in that day as it reveals itself.

If you do not have a morning ritual, then this is the one to administer to your life. The tone setting for the day alleviates the sense or feeling of being caught up in other people's dramas, or how you give your power away through subconscious behaviours and patterns. Setting your tone can be simple, it may be moving through the day with a smile, open heart, appreciating beauty around you, gratitude for health, you could decide to be more aligned with peace, have strong boundaries. There are NO limits to what you want to harmonise or resonate with each day.

Day by day, you choose something that you can align with, and this feeds your 'frequency', assisting you to 'hear' the vibrational energy you are.

Only YOU have the true power to navigate your days no matter what the environment throws at you. Your answer or response can be governed by your daily 'tone'. Some days it can be really difficult to set a tone, we have our ups and downs. On those difficult or challenging days, set a tone, to be kind to you, or perhaps set the tone to be 'calm'.

With a conscious breath and as much magic as you can muster, make a choice about how you are willing to participate in your day, exhale and ground that in.

At the end of the day, as your feet lift off the floor to rest for the night, remember to be grateful for the steps you took in offering your choice of you to the world, and how it responded.

DECLARATION

Today, I radiate the divinity that I am, in all directions and all dimensions.

ACTIVITY

Intention:

To consciously engage in your life.

Action:

- Set an alarm 30 minutes before your usual wake up time
- When you first wake up, take three deep connected breaths, while stretching your arms and legs, turning your neck from side to side, becoming aware of your surrounds. Luxuriate in those first few moments

- Thank your body for a restful sleep, for its ability to move and all the functions that take place without you thinking about them

- Give yourself a positive thought for the day, and set an intention before you put your feet on the floor

- Create a morning ritual that you engage in daily...non-negotiable (meditation, journaling, quiet space, daily motivational read, uplifting music, sacred chanting, mantra with mala, wander around the garden, or a 10-minute walk away from the front door, then 10 minutes back again)

- Stay away from techno stuff for 30 minutes upon arising

- If you are an over thinker and a busy bee, write out the list of things you desire to complete in the day

- Make sure you give yourself some time through the day to check in with self

INITIATIONS...

SEE ALL THESE energetic changes and our inner world shifts as initiations. This is a massive time on the earth as an awakening process is gathering momentum. Are we ready, do we know what is required as a new human on a new earth? We look around for examples or information, and we keep being told...go within, listen. We are being pushed through an initiation process to help us birth parts of ourselves that have been hidden, suppressed and forgotten.

When you look at the ancients, even indigenous cultures today, there are milestones in their life story that are matched with initiations, 'Coming of Age'. These actions take a person to the next level of their evolution, growth and responsibility in their community.

The collective consciousness we are all living in right now is being initiated to a new Coming of Age for humanity.

Initiations present when we are ready to change,
need to let go, purify, clear and cleanse—finding
a new level of courage, facing a test knowingly
in order to align with our new role.

As with all initiations, if we are not prepared, there will be discomfort and levels of fear, yet we are being moved towards another aspect of who we are. The indigenous cultures are richly blessed with initiations ceremonies that mark the move from one way of being towards another.

In our busy western world, we have lost that connection, so we often fall into new roles in life unprepared, not sure what is expected from us, bumbling along doing our best to show up, and many times in total confusion as to what is required. Our young women have a physical initiation. They start their menstrual cycles. This comes with conversations about the responsibility they now have towards their body, their sexuality, pregnancy, mothering etc. While people around them have an understanding as to their 'moods' (oh you know, hormones!).

Well, boys have hormones as well! In our culture there are no rituals, no initiations, no ceremonies to guide them, to show them what the community requires of them as men contributing to life. What we do have in this western lifestyle is 'troubled youth'… young boys/men doing risky things, to prove themselves as men. Their physical transition is obvious, yet not as embodied as young women's. Some of these actions are not socially acceptable, may be destructive, but there is a level of courage/bravery required to carry them out…this is what initiations are truly about, finding a new level of courage, self-belief, self-awareness and owning more self-responsibility.

If we can look at challenges, issues, troubled moments as little invitations towards initiations, the invitation to step over the threshold into the unknown, we may see we are capable of more than we knew.

Taking the steps one at a time, having mindfulness and utilising it, being non-reactive, feeling your way through things, allowing courage to find its way into your life, trusting your inner world while connecting to it, and creating some small rituals for a new reference point, then, that proverbial stepping over the line into next stage of life, will support each of us as we awaken into this new level of who we are becoming. Once the initiation process is underway, the activations begin. The new levels of uniqueness and divinity, clarity, purpose and potential are available, for us to own, and work with.

These are indeed exciting times for us all, the new human, new earth, new world is being born through the initiations we are all experiencing. Our role, once we have moved through it, is to actively engage in the new aspects of self.

DECLARATION

Today I courageously take action aligning with my soul's purpose and becoming who I am here to be.

ACTIVITY

Intention:

To create your own simple, step over the threshold initiation process.

Action:

- Get two pieces of A4 paper, or if outdoors get a stick to write words in dirt/sand/pebbles/grass

- Utilise whatever you have around you (a long stick, broom handle, string, rope, anything) to create a line, even draw a line in the sand or dirt

- On one piece of paper, or in the earth, write the word that you are ready to step away from (fear, limitations, struggle, insignificance, distractions, lost)

- On the other piece of paper, or in the earth, write the word of what you are stepping towards (courage, unlimited, success, ease, valued, focus)

- Stand on the side of the line that has the word you are stepping away from

- Take a big deep breath, feel all of that awareness of how uncomfortable that thing is in you... then when ready, look at the word on other side of the line, exhale and step over the line

- Take a new breath on the side you are moving towards and say, 'I am now ready to initiate the change towards this aspect of me.'

- Stay there and see if you can get a feel for or imagine that new aspect or role

- Step away from the whole thing with a blessing of gratitude for all that you are becoming

CLEANSING...

STAGNATION, FEELINGS OF being blocked, obstacles stopping you from living the life you want can affect all areas of life. Making sure we tidy up, clean up, clear things out is the remedy.

How amazing does it feel to walk into your home after it has been cleaned? It feels better, the vibration is lighter, there seems to be a sparkle that makes us smile and feel really good.

Clean up the energy in your home environment. We clean up our homes the usual way, sweep, wipe down, mop, vacuum, pick up, tidy up and generally do our best to have a clean place to live.

When was the last time you cleared up the energetics? Our energy body can collect lots of toxic energy as it moves through life, as most of us are unaware, not paying attention to how we feel when things are occurring, more intent on getting things done, finished and sorted.

Simple processes can create a huge shift in energy, which like walking into a clean home, helps us to feel clearer, brighter, lighter and more spacious.

We are all aware of decluttering, simplifying, getting rid of excess, and how great does it feel to have space around you! Cleaning up your environment energetically can bring more space for you, I LOVE how my home feels after a good smudge out...it's like it sparkles with goodness and high vibes.

There are times when we are stressed, or perhaps we have visitors who are challenging, negative, even hard work. We can love them, yet there are residual fragments often left behind, the emotional triggers, the judgements, the withholding of speaking up, perhaps being annoyed and a myriad of energetic disturbances.

We know how it feels to have people around who are heavy, and how it can be depleting as we are required to hold our energy self higher to not be sucked into a downward spiral. I know there are times when I feel SO tired...not from taking on what another person or situation is about, but purely from my awareness working to keep me in my own frequency.

Creating strong boundaries is one of the most powerful ways to keep your energy field strong.

We have a front door that we open to allow people in and out of our home. We need to look at having a door in our energy field, so we get to choose who can be close to us and who has no access.

Clear boundaries are not about keeping things OUT of your life, it is all about knowing what supports and sustains you and taking responsibility through discernment to allow in those people, situations, that are respectful and aligned. Keeping your energy field clear and clean is having a simple and strong set of boundaries.

A great way to keep your environment clear and charged with great energy is to smudge. I LOVE the aroma of the smouldering smudge stick, which is dried sage. Using incense, smudge, Palo Santo, frankincense or sandalwood connects you to ancient rituals that have been carried out for eons, while bringing a clearing to your space.

Some of us really need our workspace to be cleared, yet it is 'socially unacceptable' to be waving a smoking piece of wood or herb while we have smoke detectors on alert. So how to combat that...you can create a smudge spray, have a bowl of salt tucked under your desk, even have candles going if allowed, or aromatherapy diffusers or a bell.

Regular clearing of your own energy field, and your living and working space, gifts us clarity, focus, even more energy to enjoy our own life. Keeping your environment clear and clean supports you as you work to keep your own personal frequency high.

DECLARATION

Today, my personal vibration is clear, expansive, purposeful, valued and high. I am willing and prepared to do what it takes. Show Me!

ACTIVITY

Intention:

To smudge your home, body, office, environment. Activate your light within to clear your energy field.

Action:

- Place some salt bowls under desks or drawers; take a saltwater bath or swim in the ocean; use saltwater scrubs by mixing together finely ground Himalayan salt, coconut oil and a good quality essential oil. Rub over your skin then jump in the shower

- Engrave 'positivity' or 'high vibe' or 'clear this space' into a candle, then burn everyday; it will help clear up negativity quickly

- The crystal citrine is fantastic for clearing negativity. A great asset to an office, desk or space when thinking tends be peppered with negativity. Place your hand on the crystal and ask that all negativity be removed

- Close your eyes, place your hand over your heart and state, 'I invoke the light within to clear my energy field in all directions and dimensions'

- Breathe with that powerful intention for a few moments

HEALING...

MAKE YOUR OWN healing a priority. We can be stuck with self-pity, comparisons, feeling lost in our direction, lacking clarity or confidence, sitting in uncertainty, yet worrying about what needs to be done. This is normal and uncomfortable as many are letting go of what has been our framework.

Never before have we been pushed so fully to let go and see who we are.

One of the things I am seeing consistently with clients is the 'awareness' of giving up the struggle, the striving, the pushing. The receptivity of being open armed, open hearted and open minded seeing what is aligning and arriving. This is different and all that we were will resist this, it goes against what our mind and ego knows. It is the stepping away from control towards a level of flow.

Are you a person who is constantly seeing the negative; the problems. Perhaps you dwell on the same scenario all the time, sharing it with everyone yet not prepared to make changes. Maybe you engage in rumours, or feel helpless or you are comfortable being in the victim role.

Most of us, at some time in our lives, have played these scenarios out. Some learn way faster than others; change their thoughts, outlooks and actions to create a different life.

Some still play those roles as it is comfortable on some level, it can be an identity. 'If things change, then everything changes' can be quite a daunting thought for some people. There is a preference to stay in what they know. They may lose friends, as people move away not wanting to engage in the repetitive stories.

Wayne Dyer so eloquently said, 'miracles are a change in perception'…so change a perception and you are on the healing journey.

Yes, I can hear some of the questions. What about people who are stuck financially, emotionally, maybe in situations they feel helpless in? What can they do as often there seems to be no way out?

Ok…nobody has control of your thoughts except you. Nobody can take your uplifting thoughts, energy, imaginations and intentions away from you. You can always seek help.

To start any process of healing, we must engage in awareness. As awareness rises, we have the space to question our repetitive thoughts and behaviours. If you want to raise your happy vibes or move away from feeling helpless and towards the journey of healing, then start with your own thoughts. Lift them to something a bit lighter, more positive.

No matter how desperate a situation is, there is always a moment of opportunity to feel slightly better. A kindness shared, a gentle hug, a consideration, perhaps a few words of encouragement can be enough for anyone to see a glimmer of hope.

The bottom line is you have to WANT to heal, to change, to create something that will ultimately feel better. I am NOT talking about mental health issues here (depression, addictions, etc.) Those are complex issues that require a different approach.

Ask yourself these questions:

- Do I want to feel like this every day?
- What can I do to feel better?
- What thoughts can I change to something easier, something higher, something with a positive outcome?

Think about being at a red light. You come to a complete stop…your mind wanders, you forget where you are, you are day-dreaming, over thinking, playing out the 'he said, she said' scenarios, when suddenly a car behind you honks loudly, bringing you back. It is a 'wake up' nudge—the sound of awareness—you start to drive away with a cautious movement until you can gain speed and be back in the flow. Healing is a bit like this… wake up, regroup, reset, ground, set your direction, balance and take off.

Right now, humanity is going through unprecedented evolutionary changes. We are breaking out of something that has kept us constrained and we must find our way forward with new vision, until we have aligned and are up to speed. So healing is paramount, and it starts with awareness.

DECLARATION

Today I know I am whole, complete, vibrant, healed and energised. My mind, emotions body and soul are connected and healthy.

ACTIVITY

Intention:

To feel better about what is happening.

Action:

- Journal or meditate with this statement, 'I am not wounded or broken, I am in my process of healing and I take responsibility to change what is required'

- Book in for some reiki or energy healing

- Play with Oracle cards. Shuffle the cards and ask, 'What is required in this situation to initiate healing?' Then select a card

- Find a close friend and talk things out

- Ask for the most aligned way to heal the situation to arrive in your life

OWNING...

EVERY DAY IS a new life. Sometimes way easier said than done. Human nature with all our ego, inner judgement, needing to be right, getting miffed or pissed off, even feeling deep anger, will hang on to all the issues, upsets, insinuations, critiques of self and others while we try to think, over think and obsessively think our way out or through them, which keeps us living in the past, not in the beautiful present of this moment. How is it working for you?

Imagine for a few moments the reality. To open your eyes at the start of each day with a fresh awareness, to open your heart to your recognition of a brand new day, which is filled with potential and possibilities, to have a clear mind ready to create what is imagined or inspired in any moment during this new day...to embrace the day as a whole new life...how liberated is that!

We can aspire to that, we can have moments, maybe days, to really be in this beingness. All the things that keep us living in yesterday, last week, last year, even 10 years ago are our thoughts and how we felt wronged, insulted, disrespected, devalued and all the other crappy stuff we get attached to. None of us like being victimised, lied about, humiliated or even put in our places, so we immediately bring the ego army in to fight back.

Let's try this! What we have going on within us is our own stuff, what someone else triggers most often is our own stuff, what we hang on to is our own stuff, what we react to is from our own stuff, what we offer is from our own stuff. Our minds attach to all the intricate what ifs and maybes, making more of something than it really was. All our perceptions, beliefs, patterns, conditionings have become our own, even though they have been ingrained in us from family, life, education and experience. We tend to own and then live from the experience of all those layers, labels and illusions of who we have been told we are. Do you see the common theme? OWNING!

We own it, and for some reason, we like to wear some of our crap like medals or crowns. How we discuss issues with others and our actions we take in retaliation, revenge, or simple payback, the things we do to seemingly save face, keep our illusion of power, which in many cases is really our ego in a happy place, or maybe a righteous place.

Living each day as a new life requires us to own our stuff, understand, respect, observe, find the lesson and do what we can to let it go.

The more we can create spaciousness in our inner world, the more we can find things that pull us away from that place of knowing and deal with them, the closer we are to living each day as a new life. It is a constant work, a mindfulness that is ON all the time.

DECLARATION

Today I embrace the new energy and align with my highest outcome. I choose to be present.

ACTIVITY

Intention:

To visualise light to renew, uplift, heal and cleanse.

Action:

- Hand on your heart, close your eyes, breathe
- Visualise breathing from your heart to the energy centre above your head called your soul star; see this as a brilliant crystalline white light sphere
- Inhale at heart
- Exhale up to your soul star
- Inhale at soul star bringing that white light down towards your heart
- Exhale to your heart
- Repeat this for five rounds
- When you land back in your heart, visualise that white sphere moving down the line of energy to your heart. Once there see the sphere expand with each breath until you are inside it

- Command the light in the sphere surrounding you to fill every cell, every organ, every energy body, all parts of you seen and unseen

- When you feel complete allow each breath to shrink the sphere back to heart space

- Ask a question while the sphere is still lighting up your heart. When your answer is received send the sphere back to the soul start above your head with an exhale.

- Take a deep breath then open your eyes

BEING...

FLUCTUATIONS OF YOUR beliefs will happen. Humanity, earth, collective consciousness is in transition and transcendence. We can be listening to our inner world all we want and following the heart whispers, and gentle shoves, however, we will have days where we wonder why, as the old beliefs bubble to the surface in an uncontrolled way. Remember you are not just doing it all in your own life, you are doing it for the collective.

Our species has endured eons of suppression, oppression, repression and we have forgotten what we are truly capable of, what we can be. As things arise, holding the thought of when you are kind and gentle with those old beliefs in you, you are better at moving it through the collective.

You are responsible for you; you are responsible for all that you offer into life.

We can surrender and observe, go into acceptance and allowing. We can resist or berate ourselves, as we ought to know better by now! Have you ever asked yourself? 'After all the work I have done, I can't believe this is STILL showing up!' We can fall into a deep funk with a massive *kerplunk* while the resistance to what we want to do plays out, almost taunting us to give up.

You are shifting the old patterns on multi-dimensional levels. It can seem never ending, it can seem eternal, BUT each time it gets easier. Each time you can go more into an observer or witness role, and deal with the situation from an 'overview', and each time you can respond differently.

It is natural to have the ups and downs. We can appreciate the highs, we can reset in the lows. All we are doing is following the cycles of nature…expand, contract, grow, rest, birth, death, full, empty, awake, asleep.

As with any change, we have to get used to new habits, thoughts, ways of doing and being. In the down times, you are responsible for you. Take the easy way and give up, or take another way and know this shall pass, as do all things. Sometimes when things seem rough, change your environment, down tools, up the ante with your own space, check out into nature, go for a walk, get a journal and write it all out, dance, move, sing, swim, the movement will get the energy flowing.

There are times when we just need to have some time out from all the doing and thinking. One of my favourite things is to sit under, or more often, in a tree. Where in an instant I return to my youth, when I would stare at the movement of the wind through the leaves, perhaps looking at clouds…having nothing but that to entertain me.

In the big picture, the things we are worrying about and dealing with are relative to each of us only. Our beliefs, resistance and restrictions are our own reminders to keep evolving. If we can feel really crappy when we are doubting ourselves, getting frustrated at our lack of change, that is a fabulous reminder and starting point. Your soul has to deal with certain themes in this human experience; YOU chose them, and they will repeat in various forms until you are totally mastering all of you. That may take lifetimes. Once we embrace that, the issues are only seen as another resting point, a moment to regroup, find the next way forward with a kindness and gratitude for the lesson showing up, we don't tend to linger or drown in the old stuff. We bear witness, we choose something else, the higher awareness of what the situation is asking from us. Don't feel too bad when these recurring things arise…accept they just could be your road sign for the next part of your life.

DECLARATION

Today I align with the flow of synchronicity to move through my life with ease and grace. I take action on all the signs.

ACTIVITY

Intention:

Look for the synchronicity, the signs, the messages to assist you in choosing higher quality thoughts and actions to upgrade your awareness of life.

Action:

- Go for a walk, find a tree you connect to and sit with it
- Put your feet on the trunk, or sit with your back against the trunk
- Offer gratitude to that space
- Close your eyes and just allow yourself to be supported or held by the tree
- Sink into it; breathe with it
- Allow yourself to be…no time constraints
- Offer gratitude to the challenges showing up, and consciously look for the gratitude, the blessing, the teaching as everything happening to you is FOR you

PERSONAL POWER...

KNOW AND OWN your power. When I started on this awakening process towards wholeness, ascension, enlightenment, oneness, I used to think, or maybe I was subconsciously being told, that I needed things to increase my abilities. I invested in many courses and workshops, seminars and classes, bought bucket loads of crystals, which by the way I do absolutely LOVE. I just had to have the latest new age paraphernalia in the hope that I would feel more empowered, more complete, more unique in what I was offering.

Such is the belief when we want to make a difference and we are gung-ho on having all the tools to assist others and ourselves. There is nothing wrong with doing all that; as I understand, it is all part of the 'remembering process' for our human awareness. Utilising objects, learning information is all part of the reminder process to wake up the wisdom from internal knowing and deliver it into the conscious life. What we must remember is that these things are not more powerful than us.

We have forgotten our true power and these objects or external gadgets can instil that memory or feeling. We can gain confidence in our skills, offerings and service by standing behind something we think has the power to change lives.

Over the years I have witnessed, and participated in, this belief of something outside of me having the power to heal, cure, bring abundance, change lives, lift your energy, bring in your soul mate, get that new job. We all go through that, looking for instant gratification. Holding faith that some object that has been activated and promises to deliver solutions to all of life issues, will be the answer. Sure, things have energetic influences and impulses, but the real power of change, healing, attracting into your life what you desire, need, deserve rests at your own choices, attitudes, intentions and beliefs. It is YOU!

Your own knowing, your intentions, your desire, your willingness to do the inner work...let me repeat that, your WILLINGNESS to connect within by doing the inner work. I am not saying chuck out all your favourite things, what I am asking is, 'Do you believe they are more powerful than you? Or do you believe they assist in remembering the power that you are and own?' I have been wrestling with this realisation for the last few years and was given the experience to place my beliefs where my heart and soul are.

A while ago, the office I saw clients from was sold. My inner knowing said, 'Don't look for another place, go to what you love'. Nature is my place of great sanctuary, and I like to take wisdom from what is around me. I started to see clients in natural settings... no props, no table, no crystals, nothing apart from the person I am with. What happened? Freaking magic!

Big magic, big breakthroughs.

What I had been coming to grips with in my life showed me the real power in any session, or any interaction with another person, is the frequency, the current of energy that is ignited between two people in complete presence. What happens is exactly the same. The things I used to have around me were my energetic crutches, which I believed on some level were responsible for some of the crazy woo-woo. In fact, it was each person's own re-membering, own response, their own energetic highest healing self, delivering what they were ready for in that moment.

Personal power is a vessel of great containment of you. When we diminish ourselves, lessen our worth or value, disrespect our principles, or boundaries, we are disempowered. We have given power away; we have played into the not enough belief in the collective consciousness.

There is nothing wrong with saying no, or standing up for yourself, or having boundaries, or asking for respect. There is nothing wrong with having a trailer load of crystals, feathers, and oracle cards to play with if you are doing your own inner work. If you are waiting for those things to make you whole...GOOD LUCK with that! It's your call.

DECLARATION

Today, everything I need to know I already have within.
I am my sovereign soul, listening to the wisdom I have
and following through with positive action.

ACTIVITY

Intention:

Courage is an inner experience, baby steps that build gently just by following what feels right for you. Work on cultivating courage. Know what is true to your heart. Know that you can change anything in a moment.

Self-acceptance will always fill your personal empowerment tank. Deal with the discomfort by finding ways to move through whatever is there, more often than not, the sense of discomfort is resistance to something new.

Action:

- Close your eyes for a few moments
- Really feel into your inner world and body
- Step into your personal power, or empowerment, and feel what happens internally...do you feel your energy resist or contract, or fear arise?
- Ask yourself, 'Is there a deep belief about power equating to destruction and corruption?'
- If you feel the answer is yes. Then let us turn the word power into courage
- Take action when you hear your intuition
- Celebrate your little steps...each one is huge towards the final story

BREATHE...

TAKE A BREATH, relax into you, even if for a minute, you deserve it. With so much energy pumping in and around us as we all participate, whether consciously or not, in the evolutionary process of life and earth, remember to take pause sometimes.

Close your eyes to the world, visit your inner self and be appreciative, grateful and thankful for all that you are experiencing, doing, showing up for, looking towards and embodying; and all that you have moved through and beyond.

Many people are still unsure of what their personal soul growth plan is, even though we created it long before we physically arrived on earth. However, taking a step towards something you want, something that you know makes you happy, in many cases can open up the pathway.

The first thing we do when we are born is inhale, that is an anchoring, a commitment to be here, our soul is earthed. The last thing we do when we die is exhale, that is when our soul leaves our physical body. Our whole life in the story of the universe is one breath. Yet in our everyday life, each breath is a lifetime.

***We can change anything within a breath; we can
create anything in a heartbeat.***

Connecting to our breath, understanding the power to breathe
our life through choice, thoughts, actions and words is a gift beyond measure. There is NO rush, there are only opportunities to
connect and follow the internal wisdom, however that is entirely
up to you, it is your responsibility.

Taking moments in your day, to connect in and breathe, allows for restoration of self, to view what is happening. It can be
easy to get overwhelmed, lost or even forgetful of checking in
with your soul as we meet deadlines, entertain ourselves with
distractions, fall into meeting other people's expectations, get
busy doing, doing, doing.

Your soul needs a breath, acknowledgement, space in order to deliver your inner knowing to the surface. There is a great
sense of comfort, like a huge mother hug, when you feel your
soul close, when you can lean into it, listening to the inner language that is yours alone.

Get used to it. Practise it. Feel comfortable. Just like going to
the gym to get a great six-pack or abdominals, you have to show
up, engage, practise, then repeat…daily! This is your soul you are
visiting, it is your inner knowing, it is your guidance system, it is
your compass, it is your home.

Think about when you are away on holidays, even though you
could be in an exotic place, having fabulous experiences, when

you arrive home, to your place of residence, your little sanctuary, there is a sense of relief, a letting go, a feeling of deep comfort after your journey as you plug back in to your world of safety. That is what it can feel like when you are taking those brief but regular moments of time out in your day-to-day life, reconnecting to your soul with awareness and listening deeply.

DECLARATION

Today I embrace every inhalation as a new beginning.
I let every exhalation release what is not for me.
I breathe my life into the wholeness I AM.

ACTIVITY

Intention:

To practise deep rhythmic breathing.

Action:

- Close your eyes and put your hand on your heart space
- Take a deep breath in, hold it then exhale
- You can add words here if you have specific things you are addressing
- Inhale relaxation
- Exhale stress
- Inhale calm
- Exhale chaos

- Inhale peace
- Exhale agitation
- Inhale expansion
- Exhale restriction
- Inhale happiness
- Exhale anger
- Inhale quiet
- Exhale busy
- Repeat this for a few minutes, as many times a day as you want

OR

- Close your eyes
- Inhale for the count of four, hold for two,
- Exhale to the count of four, hold for two
- Repeat 10 times

This is very calming, steadying, soothing and relaxing.

CLARITY...

WHAT YOU SAY matters and sets chains of action off. We have all heard the saying, 'Be careful what you ask for, you just might get it'. I have always found that irritating. There is an undercurrent of fear, to make you think twice, and perhaps dilute or restrict what you are asking for.

When you hear a person say, 'Be careful what you ask for', it sounds like, 'How dare you?'. So, with our old limiting patterns of wanting to be accepted and loved, the desire to fit in with what is normal, we will water down our asks, to suit something or someone else, it keeps us safe, while enforcing the 'near enough will do' attitude.

Are you over it?

Years ago, I had a work colleague who went on and on every day about how he needed a break. He was overworked. I would cringe whenever he said it and hoped he would change the request. One day he rang me to ask, 'Can you take over my clients for about 12 weeks? I have broken my forearm in three places. I got my 'break'".

He really needed to be saying, 'I need a restful, rejuvenating holiday where I can fill my cup, have adventures and do whatever I want!' A clear request like that allows for movement, action, engagement, fun, relaxation, choices, wellness, not a three-month 'break' of recovery where you are limited in everything you do.

I would love to hear everyone say:

BE CLEAR about what you ask for, you will get it.

Feel the difference in that. There is a certainty, a knowing, a moment of clear intent of putting out what you want for you.

You can see this in action easily in cafés and restaurants these days. People with dairy or gluten intolerances, those who are vegetarian, or vegan, no fat, low salt, no sugar and on it goes. People, who are living with these dietary concerns, will ask and order food or drinks with a clear statement of what they want.

Imagine you are in a café, you are looking at the menu and nothing really grabs you or you can't decide, so you order something just because you are hungry. Then people come into the café, sit near you, are given the same menu, and they give their order and ask for things that may not be on the menu. The person taking the order, in most cases, will say, 'Of course!'

Now this is the interesting part. All the food arrives at the tables; you have your meal in front of you, the people nearby have theirs. You realise that you made do, or settled; whereas the people nearby got exactly what they asked for and things that weren't even on the menu! This plays out every day all over the world.

Lack of clarity creates frustration. In a state of clarity, we are certain and take action. We are able to release and let go of things as well as be comfortable when things arise that we are nor prepared for. At times, the clarity that things are as they are can be the ONLY way to press forward in life.

People who know what they want, what they like, what works best for them, what suits their current trend, will ask for exactly what they want. They are not careful, they are certain.

If we can apply that to what we eat and drink, then why not apply that same action to what you want from the universe, what you are creating for yourself, what you are moving towards, what you want your life to become.

BE CLEAR in your requests then you can enter a state of knowing. Just like in a café, you ask for your extra hot, double decaf, low-fat almond milk with a touch of froth and chocolate powder on the side, you pay your money and you wait for it to arrive. You never doubt it will come to your table. When it arrives, you smile and say thank you. Simple!

All it takes is clarity. Be clear about what you ask for and take action.

DECLARATION

Today I align with my full capacity to be clear
in all aspects of mind, body and soul.

ACTIVITY

Intention:

Observe how you hold back in asking for what you truly want. Practise being clear by stating, or asking for what you actually want.

Repeat to yourself. Be CLEAR what you ask for.

Work with clear quartz crystal. This is the most common crystal on earth and is said to support clarity and self-acceptance and bring to you what is needed for growth.

Action:

- Place a piece of clear quartz at your 3rd eye, a place between your eyebrows
- You can hold it there or you can lie down with it resting on that 3rd eye
- Invite and invoke the energy of that piece of crystal to activate at your 3rd eye
- Ask for the clearing of any haziness, or cloudiness in your thoughts and visions to be replaced with clarity

- Then once activated at 3rd eye, breathe with intention through that crystal into 3rd eye and down to your heart space
- Take a few moments here. Trust yourself, you will know when it is complete

Thank the crystal and remove from your 3rd eye

AUTHENTICITY...

BEING AUTHENTIC. SO, this is a huge 'directive' for many seekers, people creating change, those wanting to be real. The world needs this, however what is it really? The dictionary meaning of authentic is to be true to one's own personality, spirit, or character, among other meanings, however in these times of finding out who we are, to become the 'authentic me' is like trying to win a gold medal at the Olympics, there is a lot of hard work, discipline, training, focus, breakdowns and breakthroughs.

Dr. Phil defines the authentic self (authentic soul) as, 'The you that can be found at your absolute core. It is the part of you not defined by your job, function, or role. It is the composite of all your skills, talents, and wisdom. It is all of the things that are uniquely yours and need expression, rather than what you believe you are supposed to be and do.'

Being enough is authentic.

Who is anyone to tell you that you are not? Whatever stage of growth your soul is at, if you are being you, then that is authentic living.

The biggest step towards this is to live and be in integrity with all things. How you are when you are alone, the actions you take, the thoughts you have, the practises you have in your life, are part of living with integrity. You know what aligns for yourself, you know your principles, you have a passion for the causes close to your heart and you make sure you stand up for what is right for you, no matter where you are.

We are all in various states of awakening, consciousness, doing the best we can with what we have created in our lives. Disentangling from things that are not ours, stepping back from things that are no longer aligning, moving towards connections to our soul purpose, getting closer to that sweet spot of soul or not, is each person's right and choice.

Some people will never wake up, never want to know about who they are, never accept they can make something better in their lives, never want to do the work required and guess what...if they are being true to their own character, then they are being authentic in their own way. Who are any of us to tell them they need to change, they need to lift their vibration, they need to become authentic!

There is a call to our highest potential when we move into authenticity of self...and for some people that scares the shit out of them. Authentic is what we are being in any state of consciousness. Finding your way to being authentic is about taking steps to find what fills your soul, what creates and ignites that purpose, the calling to get close and listen to your inner wisdom, to live you without approval. It takes a lot of real confronting work, some of us are up for it and others aren't.

We must remember that each of our souls, the divine sparks of universal intelligence, has a plan, a road map of what that soul needs to experience in this human incarnation. When discomfort arises, when issues challenge, and people finally get fed up, or want something different, that is their own wake up call, the actions they take or don't take is about their own journey. Sure, many of us who are shifting, evolving, want so much from our deepest heart callings to help those who we see as not being authentic, or stuck in 3d paradigms, however that is our want, maybe not that of others.

The love we start opening to within ourselves, wants to shine into all parts of life, yet we can only shine it about, we can't put a torch light into someone's face and say, 'Your life is pretty shitty, how about you make some changes?' That is NOT an offering of being authentic; that is being judgemental.

Being authentic in you, gives rise to compassion, acceptance, allowing, kindness, for others. Get on with your own soul's mission; let others get on with theirs. If people wish to change; they will ask and be prepared to do what is required. However, those who do not, could be authentic in their own personal and spiritual quest. Love them anyway, respect them always, and honour them for they are doing the best they can.

Repeat the following as many times a day as you like.

DECLARATION

Today I am worth the effort,
always have been, always will be.

ACTIVITY

Intention:

Your authentic self begins with self-awareness. What are your values? What is important to you in life? What do you really care about with more energy than other things...environment, recycling, forests, marine life, clean beaches, feeding the homeless, volunteering at animal shelters? Where does integrity play out in your life?

When in doubt, don't do anything, and if in doubt the answer is always NO. If you are being pressured to give an answer and you have doubt, then the immediate response is no. If your intuition is strongly saying yes, you will feel it, without question.

Trust your intuition, and TAKE ACTION!

When you are feeling or getting some inner knowing, then trust yourself enough to follow that thread of energy. Once we take action, we are connecting with flow, and something our soul is directing us towards.

Action:

- Keep an open mind. Watch how your thoughts resist or negate new things then reframe by asking the question, 'What would happen if I did...?

- Ask some friends what they know about you. This is fascinating as others see us differently and often more than we allow ourselves to see that

- Ask your friends to name five qualities they love or admire about you

EXPECTATIONS...

LETTING GO OF your expectations, something that is well advised, is often easier said than done. One of the outcomes of not having expectations met, is a level of disappointment when our reality is not matched, which can then take us to a place of self-judgement.

Expectation is the mother of all disappointment!

Expectations are our perceived ideas of an outcome we wish, desire, try to predict, over think, or dream up, in order to induce a feeling within ourselves. We have NO control over another person's response or reaction to anything we do, say or offer.

Many of us tend to let our minds create an outcome for a situation, something that we think we want as a form of validation or recognition. Our minds only know what it has been fed via information we digest, experiences, conditionings, patterns, beliefs we absorb from family and society. Therefore, our thinking is about what we already know. Expectations come from what we know, not from the spaciousness of the unknown.

Yet many of us tend to let our mind create an outcome for a situation, something that we think we want as a form of validation or recognition. We spend time creating what we THINK is the way things need to be, often playing out old limiting beliefs, not allowing something wonderful to arise. It is like we shut the door on potential.

Expectations in reality are imposing our limitations onto a perceived outcome.

There is no flow, no trust, no spaciousness about what may be better for the situation or person.

Perhaps you have gone out of your way to create something delightful for your partner, parents, sibling or friend. You watch the response and it isn't what you thought it 'should' be, you are left feeling deflated and unappreciated to some degree.

This is what happens...you are reacting to your expectation, or trying to control the external reaction. You had a vision, or idea of how you wanted the recipient to respond, which would give you a feeling you needed.

First step, remove the words 'should' and 'might' from your vocabulary and life! You either do things or you don't. As soon as we say I should, or you should, we have set up an expectation and there is no commitment to follow through, so the outcome will be disappointing.

When we utilise 'should', it is a request for an external action or thing to fill us or help us to feel something. Time to start visiting your inner world and taking steps proactively to create a world and life of wonderment about what could possibly occur.

Know that you have done all you can to make the event, situation, desire clear. Then openheartedly allow what else is available, what other energy could be created by this moment in time.

Instead of looking for the response, or reaction externally, whatever it is you think you need to feel, give it to you first. When you have that within you, nothing will disappoint you, and you will not be living with expectations. No matter what outcomes arise, you will know you are valued, respected, loved as you are gifting that to you.

Expectations we have for ourselves can also create a narrow field of vision, halting a flow of energy that may be bigger or bolder. We limit the field of what is available, we distrust that there is more unknown to us that could be exactly what we need.

The practical application or benefit that I can see from removing as much expectation from your life as possible, is that you will experience less disappointment, less criticism of self and efforts, more openness to what else is possible. We step into the seemingly unknown, yet in reality, we allow what is to be.

Another way to release expectations is to let go of what you think should be the outcome; surrender, practise living from the heart and not the ego so much, stop trying to figure it all out, be open to a flow that is more aligned with you, and don't take anything personally.

Expectations stop flow, limit your experience, create stress and in many cases we make ourselves accountable for how another person feels or reacts, which is exhausting and deflating. We are NOT responsible for how anyone else feels...may I repeat that loudly

YOU ARE NOT RESPONSIBLE FOR HOW ANYONE ELSE FEELS!

Let us open to all that is possible, all this is available for the best outcome for all!

DECLARATION

Today I actively and consciously align with the highest outcome in my life for the betterment of all.

ACTIVITY

Intention:

Be honest about what you want for yourself and what is possible with where you are right now. You can still have a big picture; you can still align with it, however sometimes we need to spend time creating a strong foundation with what we have right now so we can build it.

Imagine laying down the concrete slab for the house you will build and live in for next 10 years. The foundation is never really seen but everything else is held in place by it. No matter what you do to decorate, embellish, expand, or perhaps build up, the foundation is where it all starts.

Set goals and outcomes that can be achieved.

Action:

- Write a list of things you would like to achieve in the next six months, one year, three years and if adventurous...five years
- Go back to each item and expand each one to the next level
- Repeat this a few times until you FEEL the energy
- Review your initial ideas against the expanded version, which one feels more aligned
- Mindfully exercise your ability to let go of expectations
- Listen to your conversations. How many times a day do you use the words should or might?
- As soon as you want to say should, or might, change it to I will or I won't. Make a decision that starts a flow of action

MOMENTUM...

FOLLOW THROUGH WITH what you have asked the universe for. We are a funny mob, we want things to happen, we ask for signs, we do rituals, ceremonies, we put it all out there, yet when the pathway opens, or the messages start to arrive, how many of us pull back, put it off, think lightly of it, or at times ignore it, because we are looking for something specific to show up for us. Keeping the momentum going and following through is about self-belief.

The level of belief in self falters, sabotages, and diminishes as a default pattern. There is some great shudder within that happens when we ask for something, or a sign, almost a black hole that sucks the inspiration, vitality and hope, as we question our right, power or creative connection to have what we asked for. It is the proverbial...'How dare I?', or 'Who do I think I am?', or 'Who am I to be that, have that, create that?' Deep subconscious, or sometimes a 'soul memory' that is in effect attempting to keep us safe, yet in reality is limiting our growth.

The universe, your higher self, the infinite intelligence working its way through life, is working with us, not against us. When we ask for something, it will be answered, what we must do is be open to how it appears.

After all you are creating your life, consciously or subconsciously, it all comes back to you.

I have heard many stories from people about asking for what they wanted and the weird things that followed. Yet they did not 'see' what arrived as the message, or the way forward as their mind got in the way, delivering thoughts of sabotage, disbelief, it isn't what I thought it ought to be, maybe it is just a coincidence, or the best one, I will see what else shows up to prove what I have just been shown. So, I will ask again...and again. This is how many people think, they forget that everything that is meant for us, will be...AT THE RIGHT TIME!

I will suggest here...Ahemmmmm, continually asking for a sign is firstly a lack of trust, and secondly nagging. I'm pretty sure as much as the universe thinks we are a great idea, loves us, and wants to support us—the whole repetitively asking for the same thing is akin to a child nagging his parents for a toy or sweet. We are creators; that is a belief we need to embody. Then our self-belief will be our best asset.

We ask, we trust, we get out of the way, and allow things to align in the best way from a bigger picture, not from our limited capacity to see our world.

Our bodily functions do what they do, and we never question that, we never get in the way, we just know and believe our body will support us. Can you believe that your soul knows its path, and all it wants is for you to listen without doubt, take action courageously, and have gratitude for what is delivered.

It is time to let go of the disbelief in the power of you, let go of the rigid or controlled ways we think things need to be answered, get out of our conditioned mind and open to the great possibilities that we are actually delivering the messages we require to ourselves. We are creating the best way forward from a highest perspective of self. It may not compute with our limited mind perceptions, but what shows up could be the very thing we need.

Following through requires us to believe, not just in ourselves, but in the magic we create when we align or work in conjunction with a force there to serve us, for our highest potential.

What gets in the way of belief, fierce self-belief, is our mind, its habits, patterns and conditionings. I know I bang on about this all the time. You are living it, if don't like it, then do something different. Self-belief is everything. It allows us to get through our days, show up to life and all its components daily, it helps us dream a new life, put plans in place.

How do you access and build some belief in self, so you improve your freedom to be you.

First up, you have to engage with the art of mindfulness, listening to the inner world from a deeper level, listening to your thoughts, and how you speak about yourself.

The inner judge and critic is what chips away at any steps forward in upgrading self-belief. These aspects of self will be with us until we perish. You need to remember that the inner judge and critic, are only repeating things you have told yourself or been told, they are like recordings. These voices are not true, but we dance to the call like puppets on a string.

When you can hear the inner self-talk, which knocks us around, you have moments to offer a new vision or a new belief into the mix. Then you must practise that, every day, every time the old belief arises, only YOU can put the new belief in place. Yes, it takes work, yes it takes time, and yes it is worth it...YOU ARE WORTH THE EFFORT!

Focusing on what and who you are becoming is a big step towards self-belief. The next step is having respect for you. When you have that, supported by trust in self...you have a great reference point for empowering self-belief.

Self-respect keeps you attuned to your inner world, while showing the outer world where your boundaries are. Self-trust allows you to bring the true you into life every day. Then you will have a sense of belief to follow through in everything you are creating. After all, it is your life...it can be as unlimited as you BELIEVE it to be.

DECLARATION

Today, I align with and embrace my visionary self.
I believe with all that I AM in who I am becoming.

ACTIVITY

Intention:

You can change any thoughts to more empowered ones, and these become new beliefs.

Self-belief is vital to your life as it helps you vision the life you want.

Action

- Visualise yourself living as you want; get some detail into it
- For those who say they cannot visualise, then imagine. Create your future self as the best aspects of you now and what you wish to be creating and living
- Spend time training your mind to see those images
- When inner critic/judge speaks up, sometimes, not all times, let them have their voice, just listen then after a little while, take a breath and say, 'Inner critic, inner judge, you are absolutely right'
- In your limited capacity of life, however, right now my heart and soul chooses to believe this, and this is what I am doing
- Exercise mindfulness regularly.
- Create a big vision of yourself with super powers, what would they BE??

Reclaiming...

YOU ARE NEVER stuck. There will be times in your life when you feel stuck, stagnant, can't see a way forward, perhaps even feel like you have lost your way. Well, you can dwell in that place for as long as you need to, and when you are done, you can:

Awaken to the knowledge that there is ALWAYS something you can do to move on, release the stuckness, align with your way in life.

One of the first things to do if you are feeling stagnant is to physically get moving, move your body; do something that gets the energy flow happening. When you take the time to walk, swim, ride a bike, paddle, surf or do a yoga class you are changing your biochemistry.

When that is happening, you have ideas, movement; you are shifting energy, which opens you up to a flow and stuckness dissipates.

If you can remember that you can:

- Change a thought in a heartbeat
- Make a decision in the space of a breath

- Have two feet that can take steps of faith and trust every day, one after the other, faith in the process of my life, trust in the way I am showing up
- Have two hands to ask for and receive what you need, to bring them together in namaste or prayer to go within
- Listen to your own inner world and find your answers
- Set an intention to fill your whole energy field
- Connect to the grace of life through simple actions of gratitude

If you find yourself saying you are stuck, can't move, not sure where you are going…practise these simple steps reclaiming your ability to be present and creative in your own life.

Reclaiming ourselves is calling back all the parts we have lost, given away or had taken from us throughout our life.

Imagine someone whittling, or peeling potatoes, an extremely thin slice is cast off with each sweep of the knife or peeler. This is how we lose aspects of ourself through life, or parts are 'taken' from us in tiny degrees. We don't really pay attention at the time, we are too busy attempting to make the peace, or stay safe, or avoid conflict.

Over time this whittling away ends up being a gaping hole of emptiness and confusion, which leaves the feelings of being lost and stuck. We will often blame others for their power over us: bosses, work colleagues, kids, parents, partners, or authority figures.

I would like to remind you of a universal rule:

Nothing and no-one can do anything to us,
unless we give them permission.

Before we blame, look to yourself. When did you allow these external bad behaviours from others to become your signal to diminish yourself? I believe the realisation, where we OWN our actions or lack of, is the first step to reclaiming all those parts of self.

Once you start, you end up magnetically calling back more of yourself. It will take time, and constant mindfulness, changing your belief about self, knowing what you want in life, and choices are resurrecting your true self. Once this starts you feel stronger, more purposeful, at peace and ready to enjoy YOUR life, your way.

DECLARATION

Today, I call back and reclaim all the parts of me
that have been lost, taken from me or given away.
I gratefully welcome them into my wholeness.
I am complete.

ACTIVITY

Intention:

Anytime you feel stuck, get moving. Once you start to feel better through moving, you 'remember' how good it is to feel as a whole person...step-by-step you are reclaiming yourself.

143

Action:

- Set 10 minutes on your watch/phone/timer
- Then walk away from your front door in any direction
- When the timer goes off, turn around and walk back
- You have just done 20 minutes of movement.
- Your biochemistry has shifted, your circulation is moving, you have got oxygen into your lungs. You have cleared your head, opened up some space for new ideas, have some happy hormones running through you and your whole body has moved all muscles

Tests...

TESTS WILL ALWAYS appear when you change something in your life. Once we have gone through the process of deciding what we want for ourselves, and perhaps begin the actioning of this, some sort of 'universal' test will show up.

The commitment we have to engage in, to continue with any new changes, new habits, choices, lifestyle decisions, is a constant day-by-day action of mindfulness. The tests that show up, which are often disguised as old habits, beliefs, patterns or limitations will define our level of commitment, our stamina or endurance to stay aligned with something else we are moving towards.

From our school days, tests were what we had to endure in order to succeed, to pass, to be gain approval, to be considered a person of value. Those tests created stress, as so much of who we were seen as and where we were going in life, depended on the end result, the pass or fail of the test.

I like to think when the universe throws a test or a testing time at us, some part of us has actually created that so we can prove to ourselves, one way or another, whether we deserve the outcomes of the changes we are undergoing, if we are worthy, if we are successful, if we are really up for it or kidding ourselves.

Often when these recurring things show up, it feels like the 'here I go again' moment. Once you have been through that a few times, it feels like you are being worn down, like water dripping onto a rock, eventually a hollow will develop in the rock.

No matter how excited we are to create new things, change something in life or self, a test is there to remind you of where you gave up last time, chucked in the towel, walked away as you were in the process of change.

It is reminding you that you have a choice to do something different this time. In those moments of remembering, you have the power to observe your old stuff and how you responded or reacted in the past and in this moment say, 'What if I did it this way?' or 'What if I choose something else?'. 'What if I can thank the old patterns for their reminders of where I was, who I was, and then allow who I am in the NOW to make the step, to move forward?'

We can keep repeating the same scenarios, and for some people that is a comfort zone, they like it. If that is your story, then don't complain when nothing new happens, or wonder why the same things keep occurring.

As the tests arise, see them as a fabulous opportunity to acknowledge where you are now, how much you have experienced and learnt over the years.

To be in this NOW, this place, this moment of doing something different, from a confident, trusting sense of self is a gift. Thank that old habit for allowing you to move on.

Tests will show up over and over, and in my thinking, I have to ask myself, 'Why do I create them, what am I trying to prove, or sabotage?' As soon as you know that, the test is over.

Sometimes the tests are a moment to integrate what we have been learning, changing, or creating, where we choose to raise the bar again. Enjoy those moments, as you know you are about to take off again.

When we are testing our body, working out with weights, skipping, running, swimming, mountain climbing, or whatever lights you up, we start out as beginners. We train, keep showing up, improving, then as we master one level, we can go to the next.

There are days when we are so tired, or disinterested, yet we continue with the training, those are the test days! Normally, once you show up and manage to get through it, your next session is way easier. You passed the test, the moment where we give up for something easier, walk away, or stop.

Life tests us, not to show us where are weaknesses are, instead to show us where we can improve, where we can commit a bit more, where we are evolving into the self, where we have made permanent changes for the better, as these are the new reference points, or foundations for the next part of life.

Living with constant connection to your inner world, listening, taking action, creating, being, offering, sharing, moving onwards becomes the new test...testing your new levels of confidence, value, belief and trust, while supporting your evolution.

DECLARATION

*Today, I move through all tests with courage to show up,
with gratitude for the experience and trust
in the highest outcome.*

ACTIVITY

Intention:

Coping when old things keep showing up and you feel you are being tested.

Action:

- Imagine the person, energy, situation, issue or event in front of you
- Close your eyes, see any energy lines of connection between you and it
- Connect into your heart and courageously state, 'Thank you for giving me this experience, I set me free, I set you free.'
- Then imagine or visualise you are severing all energy connections, like cutting cords

SELF-VALUE...

WHAT YOU THINK of yourself is the only thing that matters. What others think of you is really none of your business. I know this seems easier said than done. However, this can become a daily mindfulness practise. Our soul's journey is to get on with who we are. The unique aspect of self that is not replicated anywhere else is this infinite universe. Whether you run a country, or run a household, WHO you are in that, is the only important energy/vibration or frequency.

The more we know our unique frequency, and deliver that into this world no matter what we are doing, it allows us to be more focused on being the best aspect, letting what others may or may not think drift away.

The bottom line is, people will think what they want no matter what you do or say. None of us has any control over that it is a freedom of thought. And none of us is free from the judgement that sometimes arises, the competition energy, even the comparisons. Those habits and beliefs are deeply woven into our DNA. We can catch ourselves and change those thoughts, which is an act of mindfulness.

Spending time worrying about what others think, whether they like you or not, whether you have delivered enough in what you do, or are, is a disempowering process. It dilutes who you are, sending your precious energy into all sorts of areas, actions and scenarios away from your purpose. And remember you existing, you being, you showing up is your purpose.

YOU are your purpose!

Allowing others to influence how you treat yourself, how you think about you is believing that something or someone has more power than you, which is the basic premise behind spells, curses, hexes and vexes.

Our measure of self is our responsibility.

What we think of ourselves is being broadcast into the world and beyond. I have heard it said that what people say about you says more about them. Well maybe that is true, but when you are in the grips of feeling like crap because someone didn't like you, it is really hard to remember all those who do.

Something compels us to seek more validation, make that person like me because others do. Then the old question starts to rise, 'What is wrong with me?' This is when you can only choose the higher thought, feeling and experience of how you feel about you.

I remember giving a talk to about 500 people. At the end, there was a queue to thank me, people got all emotional, and there was deep gratitude for the presentation. One person, I will repeat, ONE person came to me and said, 'I don't get what you are on about'. I spent the next few days beside myself…wondering what I could do to get that one person to 'like' me.

A beautiful friend, seeing my angst, mentioned, 'You are allowing one person to ruin what you gifted 499 others…WHY?' It was the slap across the head that I needed to wake up to myself.

I know I did my best, the rewards were in the gratitude, and even days later people stopped me at the festival and said how much their hearts had been touched, or they had experienced a healing. Once I let the one person not liking me go, I was able to receive the power of what I delivered.

How people perceive us, and how we perceive others is purely based on our conditioning, upbringing, beliefs. So, come to a place where your inner peace, your contentment of being you is enough.

Evolving your own soul's journey takes all your energy, don't let others try to distract you from what you are here to do. When you give up seeking approval or validation you are free, you are powerful; you can be you all the time and know it is enough.

Your soul is already SELF-validated. As I say over and over…at the start and end of each day, it is you who agrees and chooses to show up to get on with it. You determine your value, your happiness, your inner peace and your direction.

DECLARATION

State this out loud:

Today I value myself, and all that I AM. I am willing and prepared to do what it takes.

ACTIVITY

Intention:

Saying YES to you.

Action:

- What are your greatest strengths?
- What do you best help people with?
- Why do friends or loved ones seek you out when they need support?
- What things do you love about yourself?
- What ways can improve your sense of self-value?
- Do whatever you do to the best of your ability
- Create strong boundaries
- Learn to say no to things you really do not want to participate in
- Set a couple of small goals to achieve each week
- Create intentions each day to support yourself
- Accept compliments

- Accept support from others if you need it
- Delegate wherever you are able to
- Be clear

SUPPORT...

BEING SUPPORTED OR supporting others is a slippery slope at times. We all want to help others, support them in their dreams, visions and life in general, yet when it comes to being supported, we often push it away.

Feeling tired of doing it all ourselves, over giving to those around, wishing someone would be there for you, finding it diffi-cult to say yes when someone offers assistance. All of these lead to the slow growth of resentment.

We find it so easy to not accept help, as we often don't want to burden others, take up their precious time or feel like we can't cope, so we refuse offers and struggle along. However, when we give support, we feel helpful, valued, uplifted as we are offering our time and energy to a person or situation we care about. We see it as service, a gift of love.

This incongruence shows clearly how supporting and caring for others is easier than being supported or cared for.

Support is a necessary human exchange of energy.

Over the last few decades the badge of honour that many of us have strived for is to be independent. The story of, 'I can do it all' leads to stress, over work and dis-ease. It is a great aspiration but exhausting in so many ways.

When we start to live a more collaborative and co-operative lifestyle, support becomes the currency. We can do what we love and ask others to help by doing what they love. As we evolve, we are required to listen more to our soul and follow that line of energy. The idea of preplaced safety nets might change.

When you follow your soul's whispers, beckoning, callings or yearnings, you will ALWAYS be supported. Being supported is a big safety net for us all.

We have been taught to look for, or set in place, a plan b, or a plan c and the 'stage left' exit in nearly everything we undertake, but more so when attempting new things, as the outcome is unknown.

For many years, following an intuitive hunch that would not be silenced, meant having a strategic safety net in place, as the fears, lack of confidence, uncertainty even huge doubt, which are learned behaviours and thoughts, would interfere with the flow of action taken.

We would feel secure when safety nets were in place, 'Ok, I can take that step now'. How brave we thought we were to step into the unknown with a safety net in place...sort of makes you wonder if we were fully committed to success, or hedging our bets! We were breaking through old patterns of resistance, where we had to conform to the world around us, while getting used to popping our head out from the rabbit warren of security, answering the call of our soul to do something different—to grow, to evolve.

We KNEW we were supported to achieve new endeavours because we had safety nets in place. As much energy in thought and creation went into those safety mechanisms to catch us, as it did into birthing the new adventure. There was a tug of war at times with where the energy was being sent.

Yes, I want to do something new, yet I can only do it if I have something to catch me.

The potency of growth is diluted with energy going in opposite directions. However it is a learning curve, one to show us we can do other things, as safety nets encouraged our confidence to move forward.

These days with more of the population in a time of GREAT awakening and awareness, the soul's calling to be who we are is increasingly louder, echoing in all parts of our lives.

Actions to do something else, to take a risk, to expand, explore, adventure, create, align with whatever is singing its way through you, means we have to take the leap now, and we are supported, it is a natural part of our growth.

I saw this in action in nature recently. Sitting at a café, a baby swallow fell on the table next to a friend's hand. The little fledgling fluttered and flopped about, then found its wings and took off. As soon as it took flight, we gathered it was its first venture from the nest; the parent swallows were hot on the flight path of their youngster. They were the support team.

I had a clarity moment and I understood…when we follow our heart, our soul, do what we are here for, we don't need to execute the formation of safety nets in place, they will always appear. The trust issue comes with taking the first step and knowing what you are about to do, face, create, when it has been singing through you, is what you are required to do…so support will always be there. Maybe the first step in our new safety nets is BELIEF in self.

Before anyone asks questions about jumping off cliffs to see if we can fly…NO, that is not what I am talking about. We are shifting an old paradigm from *when the support is there I will take the next step in life*, towards…*when I act on my soul's calling, the support will appear*.

It means that all our energy is focused on what we are doing in the moment instead of scattering the energy towards fear-based old structures.

DECLARATION

Today I accept and allow the universal support to flow through me and around me.

ACTIVITY

Intention:

How can I be the best support to others, the planet and my-self?

Action:

- Have time in nature
- Meditate
- Massage
- Healing work
- Reiki
- Journaling
- Ask others to help with things you need

Allow the knowledge that the universe always has your back to rest in your heart for a few breaths

SERVICE...

SERVICE AND SUPPORT you first.

When many people start on the awakening journey of spirituality or self-knowledge, there is a tendency to want to heal the world, wake everybody up, get all your loved ones on board. There is an excitement of discovery and like all explorers who come across unchartered lands, the urge to settle everyone there is overwhelming.

There is even a time when all we want is to be of service and support. It feels like a badge of honour, a calling to save others from their mundane, difficult or stressed lives. Those in the healing arts are passionately addicted to being of service, to supporting their community, clients, families and sharing their skills, healing abilities and information.

This can become depleting over time, as the energy of being there for others clouds, distorts, maybe even disconnects us from what is required for ourselves, as the mission to help others becomes a priority.

We often feel we are being spiritual if we are there for everybody else, sacrificing our life on many levels. It is an ancient hangover from religious dogma, also a way of being needed, and in some cases a form of control.

Ok, so there is nothing wrong with serving others, we are here to all hold hands and hearts together. However, if you are giving all of you to being of service to others, then something in you becomes neglected. I have seen the importance of being there for others and how that can take over lives, pushing those in service to the brink of emotional, physical and mental ruin.

I used to be one of those people...my days started with, 'How can I best be of service and support today?' No discernment, no boundaries, so as you would logically conclude, you can be taken advantage of, or those you want to help, rescue, fix, support, will become more enabled. You will be there to sort all their issues, be the shoulder to cry on (and often about the same thing over and over), the person taking home the challenges, losing sleep while trying to find a way to 'fix' something that is not even yours.

Depletion, exhaustion, resentment can arise if you are not careful. These creep into your thoughts and actions in tiny increments, like adding a pebble one at a time to a bucket, it doesn't seem like much, yet at the end of a day, you can have quite a load.

So how do we remedy it? Well, to be honest, some people will just have to go through this experience. It is an apprenticeship, so to speak. The righteousness gets knocked out of you, the compassion turns towards yourself and you accept that some people really do NEED to be and grow through their own shit. The knowing that we have all created or co-created whatever is occurring in life, and the wisdom that everyone has their own journey and some will never embrace spirituality, mindfulness or whatever your beliefs or awakenings are.

They can still love you and you them, but the real healing, service and support are in the allowing things as they are to be held in a respected sacredness. The ego can take over with it's need to fix, or 'I know better' or 'let me do it' when others are in crisis.

Service and support for others consists of presence, holding space, respect, encouragement, holding that person accountable for what they want to change in their life.

Being there when they need a reflection of their obstacles, blocks, perhaps some guidance or healing, yet lovingly knowing they have all the tools to do what they want. Your service and support is the compass—they have to make the choice of direction. So, start your day with, 'How can I best be of service and support to myself first, then others and the planet?'

If you can listen to your own inner guidance, you will have great boundaries, know when to step up, know when to step back and know when to step away. When people are ready for your service and support, they will be prepared to do whatever they need, you don't do it for them.

You MUST be looking after you precious body, heart and soul every day in order to have the right to be there for others.

DECLARATION

Today I choose to be and receive the fullness of being in service and support to my soul's journey first and life in all aspects.

ACTIVITY

Intention:

Take care of your needs first.

Action:

- Volunteering is a great act of service
- Find things that you love to do
- Make extra cookies, cake, soup or casserole and gift to others in need
- Offer your time towards things that will benefit others and still be things you love doing (babysit, walk a neighbour's dog)

FRIENDSHIPS...

YOU NEED TO be aware that you become who you hang out with.

There comes a point in our soul journey where the number of friends or the quantity can be detrimental, distracting and at times exhausting. We all want to be liked and appreciated and in that mission, we often lose the essence of who we truly are, by trying to be what everyone else wants from us, so we can be accepted. When something eventually happens, a fall-out, an issue, a sense of betrayal, a broken trust with a friend, we start to remember that not everyone will like us just as we may not like everyone. That is human nature.

Some people resonate with you at various times in your life, and then they don't. The exchange of energy, the remembering, the lesson has been completed. To navigate these times of people coming in and out of our lives, the thing we need to have for self is respect.

Strong, grounded self-respect—as you get comfortable with that, the 'need' for lots of friends can diminish, you start to align with the quality of people you want to be sharing time and interacting with. Your inner measure of self-respect will be met.

There will always be a trigger, a moment when you will feel the disconnection happen. However, so many of us will bend over backwards to appease another, instead of respecting the knowing we have within self about a friendship coming to an end. The underlying need to be accepted and liked can make us go against the truth we have inside. So we struggle along, smiling and quietly rolling our eyes, doing what we think is needed yet internally wishing there was a valid reason to not be spending time with a person we really have no connection to any more.

It doesn't mean the person is wrong, or anything is wrong with them, all it means is that we are growing, evolving, shifting, and some things do align for a while as we fulfil our part of soul contracts with others. When they are done, they are DONE. It is time for the next phase.

Sometimes we are fortunate enough to have people walk that whole life journey. We have people who are on similar learning curves; there is deep respect and understanding; some invisible thread holds the souls, hearts and hands together...they are your soul tribe.

There is always a circle; our soul tribe we can create around us with those who you know have your back. Those who know you, who will hold space as you 'breakdown and breakthrough' issues in life, those who will be in your crazy moments without critique or judgement and those who you can trust with the most confidential things in life you know that it will be taken to their grave with them.

Our trusted close circle of friends is a place of sacred being-ness. Sometimes you have a language between you that no-one else understands.

Look at who you hang out with.

DECLARATION

Today, I value and cherish all those friendships that have helped me evolve into who I am today. I lovingly embrace those I currently enjoy, and I gratefully release those who are no longer part of my future.

ACTIVITY

Intention:

Look closely at your friendships.

Action:

- Which of your friends would be there in the middle of the night?
- Who would you call for a midnight deep and meaningful conversation?
- Who would stick up for you no matter what?
- Who would show up for no reason, just because you were thought of?
- Who would listen to you cry, talk crazy, rage or let you be without any judgement or need to fix?

- Who do you trust with your life, your secrets, your greatest visions, your secret desires?
- Who would wipe the vomit, clean up the mess, tuck you in, bring you flowers, hug you when you are a mess?
- Who do you have a language with that no one else understands?

SELF-APPRECIATION...

APPRECIATE YOURSELF FIRST. If you 'think' you need appreciation from others, give it to yourself first.

How often have you heard yourself saying, perhaps moaning or whinging about, you want to feel more appreciated at home or at work. Sound harsh? Well perhaps, sometimes we have to be given a reality check to wake up to ourselves. Nothing and nobody is responsible for how you feel about you, just as nothing and nobody can affect you.

What happens is we allow it, we engage, we create habitual pathways for behaviours to take over, we become reactive, disempowering ourselves by believing that if our family, boss, co-workers appreciated us more, we would feel better. That is giving all your power and responsibility of how you feel away!

We wander about wishing others would treat us better, taking us further down the 'woe is me' road and never doing anything. Putting up and shutting up, seems to follow the path of a person who feels unappreciated. How can I say that? I have been there, BIG TIME!

I had to find me to discover the 'helpless' mentality that was sucking my divine life from me.

I have helped clients, friends and colleagues with a simple yet very powerful declaration process to shift the frequency. It is a state many of us have to go to in order to build the bridge to rescue ourselves, then we embrace the lesson and freaking burn that bridge! Once you get your appreciation frequency happening...you NEVER look back.

How you feel is your soul language and your platform to take action from.

If you feel unappreciated, then look to you. Where have you not spoken up when you could have, not had clear boundaries, wanted to please others, done more than you were required to in order to feel loved, needed and seen.

We are a constant work in progress, so many things to observe, respond to, disentangle ourselves from, dissolve, disintegrate, open up to, create new foundations...and on and on it continues until we fall off the perch.

The cliché, it begins and ends with you, is exactly that.

If you want to be more appreciated in your life, then GIVE APPRECIATION TO YOU first.

Appreciate you, and all that you offer. Appreciate all the small things in life, nature and all the beauty, offerings, wisdom, nurturing, the fact you are mobile, have a job, have freedom, have food, have the ability to make change!

You may have to start and end your days with that, and like anything we do for change, we have to start somewhere. The flow on, is the energy shift you experience as you train your reactionary self, or your disempowered self, to have a new reference point of your appreciated self.

Once you start to have self-appreciation, miracles happen...I kid you not...those around you tend to treat you differently. As your energy shifts, it will affect those you work and live with, showing them how to interact and treat you. Your sense of self-appreciation then becomes the message broadcast into life, guiding others to see you and how you wish to be responded to.

As your self-appreciation frequency becomes more solid, your boundaries become crystal clear. You speak up when you can with confidence, your self-empowerment rises and in the bigger picture, you are adding more appreciation to a universal connection, educating and perhaps inspiring others to feel that way about themselves.

We are all here on earth remembering, healing, rising and what you do for you, you are doing for the whole universe.

DECLARATION

Today I appreciate myself and all that I offer. I am willing and prepared to do what it takes. Show me how that feels!

ACTIVITY

Intention:

Cultivate more and more appreciation and gratitude in your life, so you *are* it, not just doing it.

Action:

- Place your hand on your heart
- Close your eyes
- Say what you are grateful for right now
- Open your eyes
- Say out loud whatever it is around you, in front of you, what you feel right now i.e., in a traffic jam...what are you are grateful for right now...'I am grateful to feel safe in a car stuck in traffic and not feel threatened by bombs.' (I know extreme, but you get the idea
- Repeat as many times a day as you like

AWARENESS...

WHAT ARE YOU doing with your life?

Are you living your soul's path? Are you waiting for it to appear, are you playing safe, have you diminished yourself to appease others, have you lost your direction and energy? Are you plodding along until something changes, are you finding things to do until you have time, expertise and space to go for what you want? Have you lost belief in what sings to you, do you doubt what you offer, are you still playing about waiting for the money, the time, the permission, the validation?

When you start to live with awareness and bring things into your conscious world through action, you will discover self-enquiry, self-examination and observation. You must then take action. Nothing changes, if nothing changes!

I was in an audience being inspired by Elizabeth Gilbert, author, creative and wise woman. She defined the levels of what we do in life and this is a great guideline to see where you are sitting in regard to living your life—the one you came here to create, participate in with a deep engagement of your inner light, your fabulous frequency, your brilliant vibration...are you heading there yet? Are you ready to be what you came here for?

One thing Elizabeth mentioned, which resonated to the very core of me was about vocations…the inner calling, the yearning that beckons us to be. I totally understand that quite a few of us have had a moment in our lives, where the calling from within, the voice of the soul, commanding,

It is now time to get on with what you came here for.

was so blindingly obvious we fell into it, became embodied by the remembering, knowing it was the very next step that would carry us forward with meaning, purpose, confidence, complete trust, a surrender into the knowing within.

I really want to share these words with gratitude and deep respect from Elizabeth Gilbert.

> *HOBBY…A hobby is something that you do for pleasure, relaxation, distraction or mild curiosity. A hobby is something that you do in your spare time. Hobbies can*
>
> *come and go in life.*
>
> *JOB…You may not need a hobby, but you do absolutely need a job. Your job can*
>
> *be boring, it can be a drag, it can even be 'beneath you'. Jobs don't need to be soul fulfilling. Your job does not need to be how you define yourself; you can create your own definitions of your purpose and your meaning, pulled from deep within your imagination. A job is vital, but don't make it YOUR LIFE. It's not that big a deal. It's just a job—a very important and also not-at-all important thing.*

CAREER...A career is different from a job. A job is just a task that you do for

money, but a career is something that you build over the years with energy, passion, and commitment. You don't need to love your job, but I hope to heaven that you love your career—or else you're in the wrong career, and it would be better for you to quit that career and just go find yourself a job, or a different career. Careers are best done with excitement. Careers are huge investments. Careers require ambition, strategy and hustle. Your career is a relationship with the world.

VOCATION...Your vocation is your calling. Your vocation is a summons that comes directly from the universe, and is communicated through the yearnings of your soul. While your career is about a relationship between you and the world; your vocation is about the relationship between you and God. Vocation is a private vow. Your career is dependent upon other people, but your vocation belongs only to you.

Relax, whatever is meant to be yours in this life will be.

DECLARATION

Today, I align with the highest level of self-awareness
for my journey. I take full responsibility for all
my thoughts, actions, words and feelings
as these create the world I step into.

ACTIVITY

Intention:

Awareness is where your energy is directed.

There is a quote that explains this succinctly. It is often attributed to Buddha, but the reality is the quote comes from Adele Basheer. 'What you think you create, what you feel you attract, what you imagine, you become.'

Being mindfully engaged, taking time to consciously connect with who we are, the energy we are, will direct the next steps in life. What you think today will become your tomorrow. The same as what we eat becomes who we are through chemical processes to create new cells in our body. High quality food equates to high quality energy. High quality thoughts, feelings, actions and words, equate to high quality life; this is awareness.

Action:

- What is your hobby? The thing that provides entertainment
- What is your job? The thing you do to make money
- What is your career? Your commitment to success
- What is your vocation? Your unique soul purpose journey

PERCEPTIONS...

WE HAVE BEEN indoctrinated to strive, struggle, push, panic, jump ahead, be busy in life in order to feel a sense of achieving, or to even believe we are on the road to success, in whatever part of life you are at. Things are in huge transition. More and more people are being forced or are choosing to drop the struggle. They cannot see the merit in it due to exhaustion or lack of motivation as things can feel so challenging or they are feeling a deeper call to start doing something they love.

The call for more ease and flow is gathering awareness across all walks of life and in all aspects of our daily interactions.

If we can all take a breath, relax, go within, trust and remember...we have ALREADY scripted this journey we are on; all the highs lows, breakthroughs and breakdowns. What seems difficult is the human condition/mind has forgotten the divinity of this plan. We sort of got lost; side-swiped on our own pathways, following the lead/advice/social conditionings of others who we thought knew what they were doing.

From the early years we have listened to other perceptions of who we are and what we can do, we have been given ticks of approval to advance in life, or frowns of disapproval to make us work harder to be accepted.

We have fallen under the hypnotic spell of proving our value to a world governed by competition, comparisons, judgements and critiques. When we finally achieve something we want, we celebrate all the effort, the blood, sweat and tears, which I will say we do need to celebrate, yet if we do not 'seem to have' or experience the heartache and suffering to achieve something we want, we can negate its benefit, power, play it down, while believing it hasn't the same value compared to another person's struggle towards achievement.

We have been 'brainwashed' into believing the perception that if we struggle, work hard and sacrifice things, we will be successful. What if, in reality, this perception of success is survival?

Most of us will have a belief, somewhere deep, that success equates to survival. If you were able to change that to success equates to thriving, or flourishing, there could be a totally different outcome, pathway, as the perception opens up to a bigger potential.

This undercurrent of competition and comparison, which we have imprinted in our DNA for survival mechanisms, is keeping us from true collaboration, true unity, soul-connected joy in celebrating each person's accomplishments in this new age.

When we can tune in to our own soul language, seek the inner wisdom of what we are truly here to activate, be, offer, share, serve, inspire and create, then we give ourselves permission to align and live it. That is when we RELAX. We know from deep within the soul's song, this is how we are.

We know that whatever it is we are being called towards (or to birth through), will arrive at the right time, when all the frequencies/energies are aligned. Sounds way too easy? Well you did write your journey, so how about relaxing into it and living it.

Everything that is meant to be ours
will be at the right time!

The right time, isn't about our linear perception, it is the 'feeling' of what you are creating, that is what deigns correct timing!

DECLARATION

Today I choose to listen to the truth from within.
I choose to change any perceptions that are
not aligned for my highest outcome.

ACTIVITY

Intention:

To receive messages as the subconscious delivers them into your conscious mind. Once you see, hear or feel them, you have the opportunity to correct it to the truth you now know of yourself.

This can be a confronting exercise. If you can commit to this, you will get some deep answers.

Action:

- Every morning before your feet hit the floor, take a moment to connect in to your heart
- Bow your head towards your heart centre and ask, 'What am I lying to myself about?'
- Take a few breaths then get on with your day

PATIENCE...

WHEN YOU ARE waiting for something to arrive in your life that you have clearly aligned with, intended, asked for; knowing that you are worthy of receiving exactly that or better, is important. Too often we ask for something and we will settle. We will take the closest thing resembling our request in order to get moving again. We will hear ourselves say, 'Oh, that will do.'

In that moment, we have diminished our worth, and we do this little by little, day after day. No wonder so many have issues with confidence, empowerment, worth and value.

In our formative years, especially when we are learning to be humans on this earth, we were master manifesters and creators. All our basic needs were met once we opened our mouths...food, cuddles, nappy change, being entertained, taken for walks, centre of attention in most cases. Watch little kids, they know absolutely how to get what they want.

As kids mature, they expect the same instant gratification; they will do everything in their power to get their parents, or other adults, to provide them with what they want. Patience becomes something we teach them as they grow, after the initial seeds of instant gratification are well and truly planted. This can be tricky, and is a whole new learning for a little one who is used to getting what they need to survive and to flourish, on demand.

For a moment think about the times you have been impatient, when you really wanted something to happen, were you conscious of your immediate attitude? Sometimes these impatient habits are in our faces before we can think about it.

Patience isn't just waiting for something to happen or arrive, it is a space of time, where we engage in a deep knowing and faith that what we are aligning with, or holding space for, creating or manifesting, will arrive in the most appropriate way.

If it is meant for our life, experience or journey. There must be energy alignments on all sides. Your energy needs to match the energy of what you are calling in.

The biggest moment of patience is when something arrives that is nearly what you want, but not quite…do you settle, or do you stand your ground in absolute certainty that you deserve to have exactly what you asked for or better.

We often resort to 'miss-out-itis', which is a modern day dilemma. This is impatience on steroids! And some bad decisions are made from that place.

Patience is a gentle art of confidently knowing all is as it needs to be. The expectations are dropped, the need for instant resolution is dissolved and there is a deepening acceptance and a place of flow.

The phrase, *good things come to those who wait,*' has become a cliché but from my experience, it is always TRUE. Sometimes what we are required to be patient about is the rearranging of energy to perhaps gift you with something better.

My greatest understandings and teachings about patience came from the shamanic training I have done...patience simply means you have created time to do something else. When you have set your desire, goal or intention, you can get on with other things. Instead of 'waiting' for something to arrive/happen or show up realise that you have created time to do something else. The 'waiting' is the process of creation. The time to reconfigure your energy field to match that which you are waiting for, or can I be bold enough to say— what is being energetically created for you, due to your request, seed of desire, your feeling, so you have the BEST outcome.

I talk about linear time as the old world, and we measure patience against that. However, in the new world time is about feelings. When you have the correct feeling for what you are waiting for (or creating on another level), then the congruence will allow the arrival, 'right time'.

To be honest, sometimes the things we really want may take years as we work on ourselves, remember why we are here and actively engage in the evolution of our soul self.

We can live without the pause of waiting impatiently. Really, when you think about it, waiting is understood to be wasting time. So change the thought to, I have just created space to do something else, create a new thing, put another thing into process!!

DECLARATION

Today I trust that all that is meant for me in this life will arrive at the right time. I align with the energy shifts I am required to make for a strong congruence towards the outcome.

ACTIVITY

Intention:

Get used to not making yourself fit in with time, but allow yourself to be and time will take care of itself. Be present, not in the future all the time!

Action:

- Take your watch off, leave your phone in the car or at home then
- Go for a walk at the beach, in the forest, bush or mountains
- Play in the now time
- One weekend a month, give yourself three or four hours of 'green' time. No digital, no electronic, no stimulation apart from you being with yourself, in nature, appreciating, being present and playing

- Connect to the world around you, nature is not a linear time; it works on cyclic time
- Take moments to breathe with the wind
- Lay on your back looking at clouds
- Do a jigsaw puzzle
- Colour in
- Do some art or craft
- Read a book

EFFORT...

DIRECT YOUR ENERGY towards the things that matter, the inspirations flowing through you, the ideas to make a change, the imaginings of something more uplifting, the desire to live in a more aligned way with your soul's purpose.

Sure, we live on Earth, and yes, we have to deal with the daily grind, all the noise of chaos, uncertainty and fear fed to us constantly through media and negativity. However, our heart, soul and mind can live in a powerful world of what we believe is achievable, a world with a higher frequency, by simply choosing those thoughts, words and actions to match what we are.

Our real world flourishes within us, calling us to bring it into the external world to be seen.

In the scheme of the universe, we are a mere flash of absolute brilliant light, signalling our existence lifetime after lifetime. Like the lights that guide boats safely into harbours, the lights that bring planes down to earth, the flashing lights that signal us take notice, to slow down, when we are driving, the flare signal at sea requesting assistance...

We have a moment, which is this life, to be, to shine our purpose.

If the world is weighing you down, you can only answer with your brilliance. You have the final say in how you respond, how you think, how you contribute, how you switch off from negative overload, how you can uplift your own life to influence others. Sure, people will say, 'You have to get into the real world'...but you answer...'I am in MY real world, this is my real world'.

There is a universal story unfolding, and your light contributes more than you will know. So show up for it! Celebrate it, as in the big picture, our time here is like a flash. Let your magnificent flash of light be memorable, enduring in the hearts of others and leave your imprint in this cosmic story of life. You matter, and you are worth the effort.

If nothing changes, nothing changes. Albert Einstein said, 'Insanity is doing the same thing over and over again and expecting different results'. This covers all areas of life. You have great intentions of doing something new, changing a habit, pattern, belief, routine, yet you get distracted and put off starting. Then one day, you are annoyed with yourself as you are in the same groove, each day feels like another 'groundhog day'. You make the decision to start on your changes, initiate a new routine, practise a new habit, 'I am really going to let go of this old thing'. The day arrives, and before you know it, the same pattern is happening.

If you go to a gym, you set programs to work on different muscles groups, and you follow it, tweaking, increasing the weight as you get more comfortable and stronger, change is occurring. The same happens with running, swimming, surfing and paddling. You begin, you practise regularly because you want to become better at it, and each session you are getting more cellular and muscle memory, you build strength and confidence and you can stay in that zone for longer periods of time.

Experiencing change is the same thing. You make a decision, and each day you dedicate time towards breaking in the new way, so it becomes a new state of being. You have to get comfortable with the changes you are creating, building a new reference point within you.

DECLARATION

Today, I effortlessly and easily align with the flow of abundant living. My soul knows where it is going.

ACTIVITY

Intention:

Experience change.

Action:

- Change one thing each day in your routine
- Add something new

EFFORT...

- Learn something new
- Set small goals that you can attain
- At the start of each week, write out three things you want to change about your life, self, thoughts, actions, and focus on working with those things. They will soon become your new habits with a higher frequency

Journaling...

YOU CAN WISH for things to be different as much as you like, and nothing will be, unless you take action. If ideas and wishes are not actioned, they are just passing thoughts that made you feel good for a moment in time.

This is one of the reasons I like to, well I insist, that I write everything down. The idea/whim/ inspiration/ imagination then has a pathway to be actioned and embodied. The writing down is physicalising what you want. Once it is on paper, it is then a reality. You have 'birthed it'.

All our thoughts originate from energetic impulses. Scientists have suggested that we have up to 50,000 thoughts a day. These are random; what we are looking at, the past, what we hear, there is action happening all the time in the brain and mind. Each impulse is an electrical firing in the brain inducing chemical reactions through the body, which give rise to feelings.

These thoughts can be inspirations, imaginings or new ideas for questions we have asked ourselves. We can let the mind play with all this energy, however if you are wanting to create change, spending time writing thoughts down in a journal, helps us to see what is important.

Journaling has been found to be a fabulous tool for clearing out our head, being with yourself and creating space for new things to come through that we can bring to life.

As soon as we put pen to paper, to birth an energetic impulse (thought), we have just brought that energy to life as matter. It is in front of us, we can see it, it is 'alive', not just a wave of energy passing through our awareness. We have owned it by writing it down. Now we have a starting point for something we want to change, upgrade, let go of or be grateful for.

The benefits are immense:

- Clear out the head
- Let inspired energy come to life
- Receive deeper answers for issues that have been troubling us
- Wisdom appears
- Manifestation increases
- Have a better understanding of ourselves
- Relieve stress and anxiety
- Boost the immune system
- Quieten the mind
- Aligns you with goals and desires

If you are serious about any change in your life,
write down what you want first,
then see how you can take action.

It has been proven that when we write down the things we wish to accomplish, we have a greater level of success in achieving the outcome. It is like a commitment. Journaling is about you allowing your inner world to have a chance to be heard, to offer some deeper information about you, your life and where you are going.

Some people find the idea of spilling their life onto pages abhorrent. Some people fear others seeing what they have written, while others are not willing to commit to opening up to what else is available. There is always a way to engage if and when it is important for you.

You and only you have the power to begin a change process, follow it up with some responsibility and discipline, and practise what you need to for the change to become a part of your everyday self in life.

These simple ways of becoming the change in your life covers all areas. Whether you want to change the state of your relationship, job, exercise regime, attitude to life, negativity, health or laziness…then simple steps will bring change about. The trick is to stay with it, so dedicating time each day to awareness and mindfulness of what you are changing will keep you on track. Sometimes having an accountability buddy keeps you honest and excited.

Take a moment, stand in front of a mirror, look into your own eyes and state out loud,

'I am worth the effort!'

Nothing and nobody can fix you, sort you, heal you or direct you, UNLESS you want that for yourself. Whatever you desire for your life, you must know on all levels that you are worth the effort of 'achieving' it from the old paradigm, or 'allowing' what is to arrive, the new paradigm.

If you want to be treated a certain way, you have to know you are worth the effort. Applying extra time to you, lifting your sense of value, doing things that you love because you choose to, going after what your heart's yearning is calling you towards are all worth the effort.

Sacrificing, diminishing yourself, hiding your needs, does nothing to support your true sense of self. I am worth the effort... own that declaration and watch how life responds to you.

DECLARATION

Today I lovingly allow and trust my inner world to speak through me in written words bringing answers, resolution and clarity.

ACTIVITY

Intention:

See a journal as a sacred container, a treasure chest that holds all of your inner life between its covers. You can create one for yourself, decorate it, add images that inspire you, that help you feel joyous, that reflect what you want in your life.

IMPORTANT...you get to decide if you keep all your journals or not. Many people do and have made books from their prolific writings. For me, I burn each journal once it is full. All that energy is finished with; I have evolved, learnt, changed, so I prefer not to have old stuff around me.

Action:

- Each morning, take a few breaths to centre yourself, holding your sacred journal at your heart space between your hands

- Give yourself permission to write from your deepest self without censor, without judgement, without agenda

- Put 10 minutes on your timer

- Pick up your pen and write. Whatever it is, let it come across the top of page, take a breath then write with that question in your heart. Some days it is hard to get moving, but once you start you are on your way...remember no judgement

- Do not read what you are writing, you can do that when complete. There will always be a gem on these pages

HEALTH…

YOUR HEALTH AND wellbeing are paramount, if you haven't got that then nothing else really benefits in your life. Health issues are a shake-up, wake up, call from the cells in your body to pay attention to you, on all levels.

When we are out of whack, disconnected, not listening to the workings of our body, mind and soul, then dis-ease, imbalance, lack of vitality, feeling off, no energy, lack of enthusiasm will take over. These 'symptoms' creep up silently and slowly.

There are many signs, signals and warnings from our bodies begging us to do something. However so many are not listening, we are too busy running towards other things, busy with manic lifestyles, finding ways to distract or get some instant gratification moments of feeling ok, so we can keep on with whatever we are doing…coffee, sugar, energy drinks, chocolate. The symptoms nudging us to change become insistent, and by the time we take notice, we have a dense physical issue, which will take time to heal.

Start to tune into your body, take note of how your energy feels each day when you wake up, perhaps even ask your body what it requires today?

I have noticed, and many on the same path will high five each other at this, that when you finally land on your soul's path, or recognise it, and take steps to action into your daily life, your health and vitality take a huge leap. Your frequency/vibration is clear, you have a better connection to what you need to do, you can begin to feel what is happening in your energy field and deal with that before it becomes a physical issue.

If you are on this path and find yourself a bit off, recognise you are too busy, not taking care of yourself is enough for a day or two of rest, awesome food, mindfulness, nature and water. To bring yourself back into alignment fast, you should:

- Attend to your thoughts, uplifting means just that
- Attend to your emotions...understand they are giving you information from your inner world
- Attend to your physicality...it needs movement, good nourishment, water and appreciation of what it does to carry you through life
- Attend to your soul...meditate, go within, journal, pray, chant, breathe properly, let nature offer your soul the nurture it requires, be gentle, kind with self and live with gratitude

Valuing yourself means taking responsibility for your health at all levels of your beingness...mind, body, emotion and soul levels.

We can practise mindfulness of how we speak, think and show up in life. However, what we put into the mouth, which fuels this glorious body we utilise to engage in life, is just as important. What you eat and drink today becomes you tomorrow. Everything that we ingest is broken down chemically, fed to all the cells of every part of our body in order to repair, create, heal, nourish, energise, uplift, cleanse and so much more.

Even if life is really busy, we still have the final choice in what we consume; how we fuel our precious sacred physical self. Each day, make a choice of something fresh, packed with natural minerals and vitamins, see what you put in your mouth as your level of vibrancy. This is a huge step in respect of self, love for self, and valuing your power to choose what is best for you. Sure we all have times of packaged food, fast food and snacks, but treat them as the rare times that you can relish, and make choices for vibrant, energised food to keep your body, cells and organs filled with light.

DECLARATION

Today, every cell in my body is happy, healthy and filled with light. I embrace my highest dimensional self.

ACTIVITY

Intention:

This process helps us to communicate with the various aspects of self. When our physical body is in pain, or suffering, usually the dis-ease has started in one of the energy bodies. When we are attuned, we are able to deal with the disturbance before it becomes a physical issue.

Most of us are disconnected from our energy fields, and only pay attention when our physical body is affected, so incorporating these questions helps to open and connect to our subtle bodies, the ones we don't see.

Action 1:

- Each morning, ask yourself these four questions, as they will open up communication with energy bodies:
  - o Physical body, what do you need from me today? Take a couple of breaths
  - o Mental body, what do you need from me today? Take a couple of breaths
  - o Emotional body, what do you need from me today? Take a couple of breaths
  - o Soul, what do you need from me today? Take a couple of breaths
- Then place your hands over your heart and say thank you
- When answers start to arise, pay attention and take action:
  - o If your physical body says rest, then make sure you take rest
  - o If your emotional body says laugh, then do something that instils laughter

- o If your mental body says relax, then find ways to allow your mind to relax, stop the overthinking
- o If your soul says be quiet, then find some space to be in that

Action 2:

Declaration to be said when walking, meditating, driving or any place you feel is comfortable for you:

Every cell in my body is happy, healthy filled with light.

CONNECTING...

INDEPENDENCE HAS BEEN a badge of honour many people display proudly, and in the times when they struggle, feel down or a bit lost, it is difficult for them to reach out for help. The shame and judgement prevents them from receiving the very thing required to get moving again.

Being independent is an aspiration, which promises 'freedom'. It can also bring loneliness and a disconnect so deep it is almost abhorrent to seek assistance when the chips are down.

As a human race, we are here to experience and master our individual soul journeys, yet also contribute to the bigger story we are all apart of to create a better world. When we feel down or low, it is often because we are disconnected from our self or from a community.

Reconnecting to yourself can be easy, when we know what we love—what helps us to lift our vibe.

However, there are times we are processing at a deeper level and have to allow that to move through us.

Sometimes you just have to stop and gift yourself the opportunity to tune into what you need...rest, nature, time out, quiet, ocean time, forest magic. Over the last decade I have been tuning into the earth energy and turning towards the influences of the heavens as they impact the energy bodies that we are. When changes are happening, quickenings, shakings of the planet, cosmic bodies shifting or holding, sunspots exploding, our beautiful blue planet responds, which means we as inhabitants will also be affected.

We can feel lethargic, overwhelmed with tiredness, headachy, nauseous, dizzy, light headed, emotional weirdness, sensitivity, strange pains in the heart area, back of heart, some 'buzzing' sensations in the body and head.

These symptoms are enough for many of us to down tools, take ourselves into nature or off to bed for some time out. Many times when we are a bit down, we need to call someone, to reach out just to talk. The talking gives us the gift of being heard, being seen, being gifted time and having someone connect with us.

As this world evolves, the collaboration energy will become what we seek, the connecting with others will be a daily dose of good vibes; grounding ourselves into this earth and our individualised life will be nourishing, nurturing and expansive.

Being informed about what is happening on earth, i.e. solar flares, moon phases, planetary retrogrades, can also help with the moving through the awakening process, as all these energetic surges affect our energy bodies and our earth.

Inform yourself, so you have a deeper connection and consciousness to the energetics that are forging through us bringing deep change, opening up areas within to finally heal, assisting in aligning our energetic bodies to a planet in change.

I am always telling people if you are in doubt over any symptoms get it all checked out. However there will be a knowing that it is a tune up and tune in, the best way to allow it, is to STOP, have awareness, ask your body what it needs right now and follow through.

DECLARATION

Today, I connect with my higher self, and the flow of grace that is always available. I choose to collaborate, co-operate and align with the highest outcome for all, for the betterment of all.

ACTIVITY

Intention:

To stop and tune in to what you need.

Action:

- Create space to call friends or family
- Catch up with loved ones

- Laugh
- Share
- Volunteer
- Make conversation with a stranger
- Organise an outing and invite others
- Find a club or group where you can do things you like with others
- Learn a new skill, craft or hobby
- Align with your 'tribe', those with the similar soul passion
- Write out a list of the attributes you would like in people to hang out with or connect to. Write across the top of the page, I gratefully and graciously call in new friends, people or connections from the highest of integrity who also have these qualities
- When you have finished that list, sign your name at the bottom and state, And it is so!
- Place under a candle, your choice of colour, with the intention that the light of the candle sends your request out to the universe, and you are the flame the results come to

CHANGE FOR FREEDOM...

MY FAVOURITE 10 two letter words are: IF IT IS TO BE, IT IS UP TO ME.

These 10 words, as simple as they are, offer one of the most profound inspirations available. We take up full responsibility to get on with what we are here for, even if we are unsure. We can still be in the flow of 'I am my purpose', until the doors to what else are ready open.

Remember that no matter what is happening in your world, you and ONLY you have the power of choice to change something that isn't in alignment anymore with who you are.

When life gets negative, drama filled, feels chaotic or you just don't have the energy to deal with things, offer yourself the transformative magic of positive action.

Choosing change becomes the action in the pursuit of freedom to be who we really—our unique self.

You could change your environment for a while, decide to engage in something that is more uplifting, find something to do that makes you smile. It doesn't mean you are running from whatever needs to be faced, it just allows you to have some space, to see if you can find a different perception, to lighten up and get out of the heavy groove that spirals you almost effortlessly into a darker place.

Yes, sometimes it is great to sit in the shadow and face it. However, there are times we need to discern whether what we are experiencing is a habit that distracts us, or a reality that has to be engaged in. This is where we start to bring into effect the freedom to choose.

Our mind will reel us into a way of being that is habitual, we find it easy to judge, criticise, belittle ourselves or are magnetically pulled into someone else's story/drama/pain. There is always one moment of choice where we can take a positive action, which will enable a magical response, a delightful new insight, an empowering call to action to deliver a pathway towards a different outcome.

Of course, we have to deal with negative things in life, but really they are NEVER as bad as what our mind makes them out to be. Once you take a new course of thought or action aligning with something positive; you see the answer, the shift, the simplicity.

Some people say you can't be positive all the time…well that is a perception and a truth. Yes, we have up days and we have low days; that is the rhythm of life. By paying attention to those low times, that frequency will attract and spiral you lower. You want to keep going down...well good luck with that! You can NEVER be rescued.

However, you can be shown how to rise again—take owner-ship and then create those actions to bring you into positivity, up-liftment and higher frequency by simply showing up for you. You are worth the effort. If it is to be, it is up to me!

There is nothing like the clarity and freedom you can expe-rience when we choose simplicity as a way of life. Yes, it takes some new aligning and some mindfulness to achieve this state. The journey requires us to declutter every part of our lifestyles.

Overthinking, micro managing, getting lost in details, filling the void within ourselves with stuff, takes us towards a seeming-ly complex way of living. We get busy, have so much to do, run out of time, mainly due to avoiding simplicity. The reality is we all have way too much stuff around us. Have you ever thought of the amount of energy it takes to manage all of that?

Simplicity is the key to discerning the difference between what I need and what I want.

When we actively engage in the choice of simplicity, we see answers quickly. We are clearer and feel more expanded, hap-pier, at peace with life and what arrives. It is a daily practise as in this time of soul evolution we are unravelling and untying all the beliefs about what success, abundance, prosperity and doing well looks like.

We can simplify problems, issues, challenges by facing these events with a calm clear mind, utilising our breath to steady our self, be in the present moment and deal with what is in front of us, without all the baggage of our history of emotional drama or old patterns.

We are being shown it is time to return to simplicity...connect with nature, have space to be, freedom to move. Life has ALWAYS been simple, we just got in the way by complicating things from the dis-ease of 'over analysing' everything. Some time, things just are as they are...no story, no reason, no lesson.

Once we simplify life, we can experience degrees of freedom.

Freedom is not about doing what you want when you want, carelessly, without consequence. In fact, it is quite the opposite. Freedom is the commitment to awareness for all that you are, be, offer and create. It is about choices to follow your heart, yet taking total responsibility for outcomes and consequences.

DECLARATION

Today, I embrace the simplicity of being who I am and align with the freedom of who I am becoming.

ACTIVITY

Intention:

Simply life.

Action 1:

- Put the 10 two letter words on post it notes and stick them in places to remind you

- Create a sign with these words to place on your office wall, in the bathroom, kitchen or any room you frequent

- Start your day with the biggest breath, open your arms to life and say out loud, 'If it is to be, it is up to me.'

- Use as a screen saver on digital devices

- Utilise those 10 words as a mantra to initiate change, discussions, conversations that need to be had

- Write down five things you want to change, or initiate change over the next month, underneath that write, if it is to be, it is up to me

Action 2:

- Select a room or cupboard, drawer, perhaps even the garden

- Set a timer for 20 minutes

- Then clear, clean out, declutter, recycle, get rid of anything that is NOT for you anymore

- Have a few containers labelled with: library, school, op shop, recycle bin and giveaways. Be ruthless in the letting go
- When containers are full, take them to the places on the label
- Feels really great to clear things out, you will feel spacious
- Repeat regularly

INTEGRITY...

INTEGRITY...WHERE IS it in your life?

Integrity sets the stage for putting right choice and right action into your life. It helps you to quickly access your 'right use of will' according to your best thinking, your present emotional maturity and the current evolution of your spiritual awareness. Living with integrity is a trademark of your heart's intelligence, and constantly initiates the best probable solutions for what works best for all involved.

There are two meanings for integrity: one is to be whole and undivided, so being strong sovereign in self. The other is the quality of being honest and having strong moral principles.

When we exercise integrity, it is something beyond thinking. It is a state of being, a place of heart-based action, interaction and responses, not for a personal agenda or attachment but for the whole situation, and the most truthful outcome for you. The intent of your integrity is beamed out into the world and affects all.

How to be in this frequency/vibration of such a big signature of who we are in the world? It takes mindfulness, strong boundaries, open heart, wholeness, strength, knowing of self, clear communication, having the bigger picture in your heart and soul, walking your talk…and so many other clichéd and inspiring states.

It always comes back to how well we know ourselves; how much respect, value and trust we exercise towards our self, and packaging it all up with grace, compassion and kindness.

Just recently I was knocked over by an action of integrity from a colleague. It really opens your heart and drops you into such gratitude when you are on the receiving end of acts fuelled by integrity. This colleague was engaged in an event I was running, even though he had other events happening in close proximity to mine, he did not confuse the energies. He intended to give his events full throttle after the one we held together was done.

His actions healed a few old wounds within me, where trusting in the integrity of others and it not being matched led to some inner growth and self-value upgrades. The gift of integrity heals, opens you up, allows forgiveness and letting go; it holds your hand and puts you into a flow of you being enough by being you.

Walking, living and breathing in your own integrity, will attract and help you create the most aligned things into your life. And in these current times of veils falling away, more clarity and feelings about situations and people, standing in your own integrity will mean sometimes saying no…no matter how flipping awesome something sounds. If it doesn't feel right, it isn't.

Integrity is an internal rhythm, which pulses through us. Once we find it, it becomes the bass beat to all that we do, offer and be without skipping a beat.

Maya Angelou said, *'Everything in the universe has a rhythm, everything dances.'*

All of life is in a state of movement, and within that movement we find rhythms. Even a rock sitting for eons, has at its very essence, atomic movement. The slower the atomic movement, the denser things are, this is basic science.

Our human body is fuelled and filled with rhythms. Each breath is an invitation, a confirmation where we say YES to spirit. The rhythm of our breath can take us from stressed and panicked to calm and rested. Sammy Davis Jr stated in his song lyrics, 'the rhythm of life is a powerful beat, puts a tingle in your fingers and a tingle in your feet'...bet you just sang that!

Our circulation flows with the rhythm of our heartbeat, digestive systems have peaks and ebbs, even sleeping follows a pattern. Looking outside of the body we see the rhythm of the tides, the moon cycles, nature and the seasons. The more you look, the more you see rhythms moving around us. When we start to investigate our own personal rhythms, we can find a gentleness towards self.

The wisdom of knowing your own rhythm, is you can respect it, allow it to be, without berating yourself. We have high energy days where we are productive, decisive, creative, and other days where all we can manage to do is lie on a couch and channel surf.

Nature has dormant times, where rest seems to be taking place. Under the surface is a recalibration of sorts, a readying for a new phase of growth and expansion. We should look at our down days, the ones where we struggle to get going, as a time in the rhythm of our personal frequency, where we could be resetting our inner selves, having some space to rest, being truthful to what we need.

Surrendering to a natural force where a higher intelligence, a deeper knowing is at work. This is all about taking time to know you. What stimulates you, what distracts you, what excites and uplifts, which things seem to drain you or where you lose interest? These are all clues to your natural rhythm. You could say it shows you how you relate and interact to the world around you.

DECLARATION

Today I am aligned and vibrating at the highest level of integrity for my soul journey and for what I contribute to life.

ACTIVITY

Intention:

Always do what is right for you. Even if everyone else around you is doing something that feels wrong, stay true to what you know is right for you.

Action:

- What are your principles, the things that you are passionate about?

- Follow through with all commitments and promises

- Own your mistakes

- Always give consideration to things asked of you, if they align, if you are able to complete

- Feel safe and courageous when you say no

- Are you able to speak up for yourself no matter what the consequences?

- Exercise compassion for others and yourself

- Be clear in decisions

- Have strong boundaries

- Engage in your sense of self-value

- Spend some time feeling the rhythm of your breath, your heart beat, without making it anything else. Just sitting in pure awareness

- Maybe your rhythm to get things done needs some structure, some guidelines. Not rigid, but reference points to keep you in flow towards the outcome

- Fun thing...learn how to drum, you will really understand the meaning of walk to your own drumbeat

EARTH...

CONNECT TO THE moon energy; it is a constant illumination reminding us of the cycles in life— the birth, death and rebirth of cycles, states of being. We can begin to appreciate our life's journey as it becomes evident when you take time to follow the moon's journey through the heavens.

La Luna gifts us softness, the gentle nurture or embrace after we have been immersed in the masculine energy of the sun each day. If we can visit the moon at night, tune in, even breathe in her softness with intention, there is a sense of nurture, comfort and ease. She governs the waters of life, the oceans, the fluids in our body, and our emotions.

Each new moon offers an opportunity to set intentions and focus; each full moon allows us to align with releasing what is no longer serving. We need to let things go in order to create space for new things to arrive.

Do one small action each day that will benefit the world. We have all heard of random acts of kindness, I am a great advocate and action-taker, as I know the benefits for some can be a life changer.

The small actions we take each day, without fanfare, without an agenda or expectation gift us more than we can imagine as we dance in the energy of giving and receiving.

These actions can be really simple things. Pick up litter if you are out and about and dispose of it properly. There is no need to get agitated due to someone else's seemingly lack of responsibility, take action. If it annoys you, then do something.

Give a wave of acknowledgement to the stop/go workers at road works. They are there for our safety, not to make our days difficult. Offer assistance if you see someone struggling with bags, boxes, heavy loads. Sometimes people don't want to ask for help, but will accept it gratefully if it is offered. Let other drivers merge into your lane, or at congested areas...we are all in the same position of being held up in traffic.

If lost or hurt animals find you, then take them to a vet, they will be cared for properly. Got neighbours who are unwell, can't get about much, walk their pets, if you cook something, perhaps take some excess to them, take their bins out, see if you can pick things up for them at the shop.

Have a look about in your daily life...see something in the world that needs to be done...take action. Not for reward or praise, simply because your one small action can make a difference in the bigger picture. We are all in this together.

Listen to your instinct, that first moment before thought engages whenever you see things happening in the world around you. Your soul will acknowledge something for you to do. When the mind kicks in, it will bring up the issues, the annoyance and sometimes the stubborn refusal to pick up after someone else. However, your soul knows how a simple action will keep you in a state of peacefulness.

I remember a few years ago when the nuclear meltdown and tsunami happened in Japan. I was out walking the very next day thinking about it when a person drove past in a car and threw some empty cans and burger wrappers out of the window. I was so freaking pissed off when I saw that...I heard my mind go into all sorts of judgements, and I was furious that people could be so ignorant to the events of the world. Then I went over and picked up all the rubbish, popped it in the bin, with quite a few f bombs followed by idiots. At least that small action helped me centre back into peace.

Others are not consciously connected to life, but I am, so it is up to me to take action on things that are my principles, my passions, my contributions.

DECLARATION

Today I honour Gaia, the spirit of earth and send her blessings, healing and respect. I walk gently with gratitude, for the nourishment that fills me, supports life and sustains the planet.

ACTIVITY

Intention:

Each day set the intention that each footstep you take on earth for the day, offers blessings, healing, gratitude, respect and grace back to the planet. See yourself as the conduit of energy between heaven and earth. Your footsteps matter so make the intention important.

Action:

- As you walk, you can add a mantra like:

  I bless the earth

  I offer gratitude for wonders and beauty of this planet earth

  Thank you Gaia for supporting and sustaining all of life.

In the Andean culture, they offer the first part of their drink to the earth, as a gesture of gratitude. I like to do that with my last cup of tea for the day.

- What can you offer the earth each day as your contribution of giving back?
  - o Practical things
  - o Recycle
  - o Collect vegie and fruit scraps to start a compost
  - o Plant some vegies, herbs
  - o Create an altar in your garden devoted to the spirit of earth

EXPLORE...

DO YOU LIKE adventuring or are you a person who likes to know where you are going? Stepping out into the unknown or doing things we have never done before is an opportunity to have an adventure, to explore more about ourselves, to discover who we are becoming.

Too often we repeat the same things, over and over, due to comfort, we know the outcome of what we are doing. To open yourself to the unknown can be viewed as either frightening or exciting.

It has been said the universe exists in each of us,
as each of us exists in the universe.

The barrier to exploration is fear of the unknown, which translates to fearing lack of control.

Control is restrictive and limited: exploration is open and unlimited. You don't have to be a mountaineer or an adrenaline junkie; you only need to be curious.

The action of curiosity safely opens us to the unknown, as we can think and feel what is possible. The imagining can be the beginning of how an adventure might affect your life.

So, before you take off on some wild adventure throwing caution to the wind, start closer to home. Follow a road, take a few turns, go into unknown areas, get out of the car and wander. See the life around you, climb some rocks, walk in creeks, marvel at the wisdom of the trees; listen to the sounds of life, breathe, be still, feel and allow yourself for a few moments to be completely connected to the rhythm and pulse of life.

Personal exploration is easy; you do not have to be anywhere other than with yourself. You can have adventures with your inner world by tuning in.

Find some stillness. This doesn't mean you have to go to a cave and disappear from life to achieve a higher state of knowing or being. The action of finding some stillness in the day, or within you, allows for integration, births creativity, reconnects you back to your state of being, creates space to reflect, contemplate, offers reconciliation and pause. In my experience, stillness takes me into a place of timelessness.

Going on a walk of beauty as an exercise in exploration in your own area, bringing your outer world and inner world together for observation, is a gift to all the senses. Being present to what you are choosing to see, allowing those moments to touch your heart, can be beautiful reference points. We have a memory that transports us to something wonderful.

This is an old Navajo prayer that we can offer no matter where we are in life. It reminds us the walk of beauty is an adventure, a way to explore the world through the eyes of gratitude and choice.

As I walk, as I walk

The universe is walking with me

In beauty it walks before me

In beauty it walks behind me

In beauty it walks below me

In beauty it walks above me

Beauty is on every side

As I walk,

I walk with Beauty.

How we choose to see things in life is how our mind has been conditioned, what state we are in within ourselves. We can walk along a littered street and only see that, or we can look to the skies, the trees and give thanks that we have that to appreciate and drink in. Life can be ugly, with all the chaos around the world, yet at the depth of each soul is a purity of beauty, of light and of knowing.

What creates the supposed ugly is the way our mind has been conditioned to work, has been trained to behave and has been brainwashed to believe. Your state of mind determines what you see around you.

If you are feeling really low, unhappy, stuck. Then you will only see things that match that vibration/resonance, which will spiral you down lower. If you are feeling really great about you and life, then you will see all the fabulousness around you, as that is the resonance with your mind and feelings.

In any moment, for a brief breath, you can choose to see where the beauty is in the world around you. That in itself can lift your frequency, sharing it with someone will anchor that feeling.

What are you doing? You are making a decision, taking action to allow the beauty that resides within you, to have a moment of recognition through the reflection of your environment.

You are reprogramming a thought pathway; to see something more, find the gem in any moment. Some would say you can't be positive all the time. Well, maybe not! However, if we attempt to make small changes each day, lifting our view of life up a notch at a time, we could be in the creative stage of greatness and beauty. Little by little those choices by more individuals will create such awareness that we will see life generally as being pretty amazing.

We all know that feeling when a new bub is birthed, the open-heart feelings of love, wonder and excitement, the inner potential shining out as this new soul helps us to remember who we are. The softening that naturally occurs, beyond the 'learned' barriers of resistance, guardedness, boundaries and protection.

As you make choices to see life from the gift, not from the issue, you are changing your inner dialogue, lifting your frequency, resonating with something more aligned within you.

DECLARATION

Today, my open heart is full of grace as I consciously recognise and walk the beauty of my life with awareness. I am grateful for the divinity in all that I see.

ACTIVITY

Intention:

Look at life and find the beauty, search for it in all things. Once you start to connect, you see the truth of beauty everywhere. Your heart relaxes. Your soul is elevated.

Action:

- Find five ways each day to discover pleasure in things you regularly do without thought and apply the eyes of beauty to that, i.e. the first cup of tea or coffee in the morning can often be gulped down without thought
- Stop and appreciate everything about it

GROUNDING...

OUR WORLD IS an energetic cauldron operating in a bioelectric field. We have particles called positive ions floating about that are attracted to the negative ions our cells produce. Due to the disturbances from the overload of electromagnetic charges in our atmosphere, producing more positive ions, we are becoming more toxic, with many symptoms.

When we feel toxic, we are disconnected, lethargic, not feeling great, low energy, headachy and more, we often feel the desire to be in nature. Nature produces negative ions. Places like the forests, waterfalls and the beach are places we would all say we feel great once we have spent time there.

It has been proven that alchemy happens at the beach. Where the water, land and air meet. There is a huge chemical reaction that doses us with feeling better.

Why do we need to wait until we fall apart, get sick or feel unwell before we take time to fill up with negative ions of goodness?

The first thing to work on is being grounded, or being earthed. Go barefoot for five minutes a day. Take the blindfolds (shoes) off your feet, reconnect with the earth; walking bare foot or allowing your feet to be on the earth is an energising experience.

Something from our ancient past is remembered. A time where we all listened to the earth through our feet, felt the pulse of the earth with our footsteps, offered an exchange of sacred connection. Just for a few minutes a day, remember...take your shoes off, stand on the earth.

There has been a groundswell of information, techniques and industries offering some ways to earth or ground ourselves. These products make it convenient, however the best form is to wander about on grass, sand or dirt with bare feet and it is free, plus you have to be outdoors.

An energetic exchange happens when our bare feet touch the earth. Nature is offering us negative ions, the feel-good particles that recharge us, clear out the toxic residue from a life where most of us are drowning in electronic distortions, called positive ions.

Positive ions are more abundant in cities and anywhere near electronics and electro-magnetic frequencies. Think of a cell phone, laptop, tablet, television, cell phone tower or microwave. Basically, anything with a power source that emits a signal; these are depleting our energy.

Since we live in a world of positive ions and disconnect ourselves from the earth's natural negative ion field, we are flooding our body with pro-inflammatory positive ions caused by the electronics and gadgets around us.

This is one of the best reasons to get back to playing in nature where negative ions lift us up and clear our energy fields; they balance us. When you're barefoot, your body is able to absorb Earth's limitless supply of free electrons. These electrons serve the function of antioxidants by stabilizing rampant, unhealthy free radicals in your body. It's not surprising that most mind and body exercises (yoga and tai chi) are done barefoot, to establish this sort of connection.

The central focus involves 'growing a root'. Doing so allows for the opening of a pathway between the earth and the body by way of the feet. Another way to ground our energy is to eat root vegetables, potatoes, sweet potatoes, beetroots, carrots or anything that grows under the earth.

Being grounded keeps us stable, energised, balanced and allows us to have strong foundations in life. These strong foundations bring a sense of safety and security.

Walking barefoot connects us to earth. Seeing our energy exchange is the grounding and balancing aspect.

Science is proving that when people practise grounding themselves, their health improves as stress levels reduce and circulation improves.

DECLARATION

Today, I am grounded with vitality, happiness, clarity, confidence and harmony. My cells are clear, my mind is open and my heart is full.

ACTIVITY

Intention:

To be grounded and balanced.

Action:

- Go barefoot every day if you can
- Visualise a line of energy moving from your heart down through your legs and out through your feet
- See the energy lines moving into the earth like tree roots, going deeper
- Then see the energy of the earth being absorbed into those roots and being brought back to your heart
- Exhale your energy down into the earth
- Inhale the earth energy up to your heart
- Stay with this focused visual for a few breaths or a few minutes
- This is grounding no matter where you are, even in a high-rise building
- A Himalayan salt lamp can bring negative ions into your living and working space

Holding Space...

HOLDING SPACE FOR others, or even yourself, is about conscious presence, deep listening, no agendas, not wanting or needing to fix, heal, advise, judge, critique or enable. It is the conscious act of listening to understand, not wanting or needing to respond.

The reality is, we all know what is required of us, the answers to issues and challenges lay within each of us, as we have co-created them, yet over time we have lost confidence in our ability to trust ourselves. We often seek validation from those we love, and sometimes from healers, readers, counsellors or therapists... as our habit is to seek approval from others, or allow others to tell us what to do.

We then have a place to go if things go to shit, 'Oh, so and so told me to do this!' Yes, there are times we require professional help; I am not talking about that. I am offering a reminder of the power and beauty of holding space for another person, for them to reach that place beyond all the labels, confusions, conflicting thoughts, illusions, veils of distractions and beliefs, to arrive at their own wisdom of self.

Being held in that container of respect, when someone is holding space for you, is such a relief. We are totally supported to go to a place where being vulnerable is the only option. We feel seen, heard, witnessed in such a non-judgemental way, that the grace of healing is the guiding light to revelation of what is embedded under all the lies, deceptions, beliefs. It is like following the yellow brick road, the path to the centre of you, where the truth of you awaits.

Holding space is totally of heart service, complete and empowering. Whatever is happening is not about you, it is all about the other person and the journey they are embarking on to reveal the answers, for themselves.

In effect you are creating an environment for transformation to occur, which encourages healing, expansiveness, realisations and comfort.

The one thing most of us require for deep healing is to be heard—really heard.

You gift full attention to a person you are with, and allow them the safety, freedom and support, by just being there. You create a sacred space from heart to heart, soul to soul.

Holding space is not the same as giving away your energy. When you give someone your energy, either consciously or unconsciously, you're not helping them. You're trying to make yourself feel better by feeling needed or useful. You might have created a belief that the way to help people is to give of yourself, but giving of yourself is not the same as standing in your centre, allowing people into that space and then taking appropriate action.

When you're ready to be a sovereign being, not exhausted or lost in other people's energetic spaces, but radiating from your core, then you become very powerful. People come to you. They're magnetised by you. You become a master at holding space, as you know what is yours, and you allow another to recognise what is their stuff. There are no blurred lines, no energy exchanges, no taking things on for another person, no getting caught up in the story of suffering or pain. Just the openhearted I am here while you process what is required.

What they then do with the outcome of the experience of being in that energetic presence is really none of your business. You have held space, the person has got to a place where they can shift; you are done. Their responsibility is then to change, shift, evolve or not. Some may heal from the experience; some may turn from it. That's their choice.

Understand that it's not about you—it's all about the person you are holding space for. Holding space is a gift of allowing and accepting another to be, say, and do as they must in order to get closer to what they know within is their truth.

DECLARATION

Today I gratefully sit in the sacred space of being.
I offer support from this place of peace.

ACTIVITY

Intention:

Holding space, allows a person to locate their inner wisdom, find their answer, find a resolution and find their peace. All because you stayed centred in your core self.

Action:

- Stay in your centre
- Breathe. Maybe place a hand on your heart to draw awareness to your core
- Stay quiet and listen
- Listen to life
- Practise listening, then when someone requires your help, you can go to that restful, peaceful stillness and just listen
- If people are asking for answers, then ask questions. If someone is having a challenge with a relationship and they are banging on about it, listen then ask questions like:
  - Do you want this to change? Then listen
  - What do you think you need to do to create change? Then listen
  - Where do you think you need to start? Then listen
- You ask the questions, and allow the person to reveal their own answers

VIBRATION...

LISTEN TO INSPIRING music. Words, music, our consciousness, our body, indeed the entire universe is nothing more than vibration of energy. The rate this energy vibrates is called the frequency. Rocks, emotions, people and even planets differ from each other, and everything else, because of their unique vibrational frequency.

Music is a vibrational frequency, which affects our energy body. Indigenous cultures all used musical instruments in healing, ceremony and celebration. Drums, rattles, flutes, didgeridoos, stringed instruments, clap sticks, shells, even rocks being tapped together have been a part of human's evolution. Chanting, mantra, singing bowls are other ways humanity has brought music into their lives to assist in healing and raise their consciousness/frequency/vibration.

Even nature, when you close your eyes and listen, has a music of its own. The earth has a pulse, a deep hum, the wind, the flowing rivers, tides of water, even a fire crackling, the animals, whales, dolphins, birds and insects have music in their communication...it all sings a song of musical vibration to us.

Music that is joyous and light can lift you out of a bad mood. Swami Kriyananda, the founder of Ananda, said, 'music is a matter of consciousness, not taste' This means that people's preference for music is based on their level of consciousness. If you listen to music based on the mood you are in, then you will stay in the same place. However, choosing music that is the opposite of your mood will change how you feel.

Sound, musical notes when you keep going up the octaves eventually become a colour ray. Sound and light are the same thing just vibrating on different levels. Not only are you bathed in musical notes that affect all of your being; you are cloaked in colour we are unable to see.

Experiments have been done over the decades to plot the effects of certain types of music on plants. The results found that classical, spiritual and uplifting music allow the plants to flourish. Human behaviour has been mapped and the differences noted with similar results. Music affects us on all levels; movement occurs, you want to sway, tap your toes, dance, let go! Play with music and see how you feel.

Laughter is simple, accessible, necessary and healing. 'Nonsense wakes up the brain cells. And it helps develop a sense of humour, which is awfully important in this day and age. Humor has a tremendous place in this sordid world. It's more than just a matter of laughing. If you can see things out of whack, then you can see how things can be in whack.' Dr. Seuss

Laughter is one of the ways we bond with one another. Laughter is contagious and so are the bonds that are formed among people who laugh. We usually feel closer to those we've shared a laugh or two with. It doesn't even need to be expressed verbally. There are few things on this earth that bypass all barriers, judgements, resistances, dogmas, rules and regulations, one of them is laughter.

When you hear children laugh, you cannot contain yourself, you find their innocent joy travels in ripples all around them, you find yourself giggling as well, sometimes laughing so hard tears flow from your eyes.

Laugher is an outward expression of love, joy, connection, celebrating the child within. Just because we are 'grown ups' doesn't mean we have to be serious and disciplined all the time.

Break out, laugh in joy. When we feel a heart-felt chuckle, it can cure a panoply of ills. Laughter lowers cortisol levels, which are linked to all sorts of stress-related diseases including heart disease and high blood pressure. Getting the giggles also increases the antibodies in your blood, which boosts the immune system so we can more easily evade bacteria, viruses and parasites, basically raising our frequency.

In a recent study by Dr Mary Payne Bennett, laughter was found to boost the immune system by as much as 40 percent.

Laughter is seen as a survival mechanism. How often do we try to make light of something, to find the humour if situations are tense or threatening? A dose of laughter in the moment, reduces the stress hormones, soothes tension and increases oxygen uptake. Just for a moment think about all the bodily movements that are increased through the act of laughing. There is alchemy, which shifts the energy, lightens you up, sends that vibe into the external world, to 'invite' others to join in the release and uplifting feel of laughing something off.

Hang out with people who make you laugh, find ways to see the humour in situations, if you're feeling unwell, watch some comedy, have some hearty laughs. Laughter is bonding, healing, uplifting, raises your vibration, supports healthy body systems and opens your heart.

'I love people who make me laugh. I honestly think it's the thing I like most, to laugh. It cures a multitude of ills. It's probably the most important thing in a person.' ~ Audrey Hepburn, actress

DECLARATION

Today, I vibrate with abundant joy in all directions and dimensions.

ACTIVITY

Intention:

Do things that bring joy to the heart and a smile to the lips.

Action:

- Watch some comedy movies
- Have a dinner where everyone has to wear a funny hat, glasses or costume
- Play some games that create laughter.
- Hang out with kids.
- Look for the humour in situations.
- Smile a lot!

MOVEMENT...

HOW YOU HANDLE and manage any situation, challenge or experience in your life is how you probably handle all of them.

I have heard this a few times, yet when on a yoga mat, my own universe, and the teacher speaks it, the resonance goes deep and the meaning becomes a new way of being.

We often act and react from habits that we are unaware of, following patterns that we never question. Start to take notice of your actions and interactions. How are they showing up in life? For example, how do you perform at work? What are your friendships like? How do you approach a challenge?

If you are late with deadlines at work and do not pay close attention to detail, then the chances are that these characteristics can be seen in your personal life and relationships as well.

How you do anything, is how you do everything

When you apply this awareness you have to recognise, own and choose to change your habits. Which routines and patterns constantly appear in your life? Let's use procrastination as the example, one that so many are afflicted with! If procrastination is in one part of your life, then it will appear in everything.

Putting things off until the last minute, finding other distractions or new tangents to be excited to begin, but fizzle out once undertaken, our mind starts the dialogue of...'Another thing I have to finish/complete/do...oh, I am too busy and will leave it for another time'. 'Why did I start this? I really want to do other things and this feels like it is too hard to get done right now.' 'Oh, I have plenty of time to compete this, I will leave it until later.' Do any of these sound familiar?

Habits like procrastination inhibit growth and evolution, the spirit is willing, but the mind is too busy entertaining itself with the why nots, the what ifs and the not enoughs.

Once you recognise the habit, then you can change it. And like all new things, it takes practise. Just like trying to build your biceps up, you have to work at it everyday. Once you change a habit, you see that it affects everything else. Keep following the new practise; you will be tempted to waiver, quit, give up, return to the old comfortable way...that is when you need to have a bold declaration to keep you on track.

Let this choice moment be the moment-to-moment intent, gathering momentum. How I do anything, is how I do everything. Sit with that and be honest with yourself about how you can at times disrespect the fabulousness that you are by not being fully

244

present in all that you do, and from the core of your soul make a choice to change.

Get moving. Any type of movement, whether gentle stretching or manic gym sessions gets the 'chi' moving in our bodies. Chi, or energy, is in constant movement, so allow your body to move with the energy running it. The trick to raising you frequency, no matter what form of movement or exercise you participate in, is to be aware in the moment. Movement of the body shifts stagnation, gets the body functions moving, increases circulation, assists with oxygen uptake and on an emotional level can help you move through whatever is up for you.

The mind can be cleared of clutter and chatter as you focus on what is happening to your body in the moment. If you walk, you have awareness of your feet and the view; if swimming you can focus on the feeling of the water as it moves around your body; at the gym, the awareness is about the individual muscle groups; as you run, the breath and heart working, the beads of sweat, the miracle of the body at work; dancing gifts us the flow of energy and a creative expression. In these times of increased sedentary lifestyles, to create a daily action of movement is a great gift to your consciousness.

When life gets busy, you can always find 10 minutes to walk away from your home or place of business, and then return. This gives you a 20-minute walk, enough time to be with you, move your energy, clear your head, take some deep cleansing breaths, change your scenery, allow some inner biochemistry to kick in.

Movement is a MUST...if you let a piece of machinery sit for too long and stagnate, the parts rust and seize...your body is designed to move. Experience different ways; find the ones that work for your body and when you are in that space, feel into the miracle of how your body works for you, and the sensations of the environment you move in.

DECLARATION

Today, I choose to finish, finalise and complete all tasks as they arise. I am focused, clear and on track.

ACTIVITY

Intention:

Create a daily practise of moving with intention.

Action:

- Walk for 10 minutes
- Consciously breathe for 10 minutes
- Stretch for 10 minutes, if you can do 20 minutes, even better
- Join a dance class, a drumming class, yoga or pilates, gym, walking group, running group, cycling group.
- Find the ways to move that you enjoy then get moving

RISE…

BUZZWORDS COME FROM all across the world and enter our mainstream vocabulary once a tipping point of understanding is reached.

Frequency, personal vibration, quantum science, soul work, mindfulness, energy medicine and law of attraction are all concepts, teachings and ideas, birthed from visionary people aligning and practising these ideals, who then share them with those ready to embrace the new human we are becoming.

All of humanity is in an evolutionary process. You only need to look at the digital devices in our daily life to recognise how life today is totally removed from life 20 years ago. Everything is changing; even our priorities are different today from those of our recent ancestors.

Thanks to technology, the understandings are now delivering proof of these ways of being. The fact is —if nothing changes, nothing changes!

As the energy of the planet is lifting, it has its own evolution; each living being is under the same influence. We are required to change ourselves, to create a world that is more harmonious, just and compassionate. We do not attempt to climb the mountain to make change; we start at the foundation, which is each of us individually.

Opening up with awareness to what we are here for, our true soul purpose is the gift of us in this earthly vibration.

Ok, if everything is energy moving at varying speeds to create matter, it reasons that we are vibrational beings that have a unique frequency, not replicated anywhere else in the universe, to attend to daily. Who we are is a culmination of our thoughts, actions, words, feelings, history, beliefs and conditionings.

To elevate ourselves, or to rise to the next level of life, we are being shown how to lift our vibration, or lift our energy to create the world we want to live in. Remember, when things were denser, heavier, we took stairs to go to the next level in a building, which required a lot of energy. These days we have lifts we can go to other floors really quickly. Apply this analogy to your own personal vibration or frequency.

The information available these days repeatedly and emphatically tells us that we have all the answers within. Tuning in and listening is the equivalent of taking the lift to the next level!

The best way to raise your own vibration, to act from a conscious based way of living, is to engage in self-responsibility. How you respond, react, think, feel and interact always comes back to you. Staying positive, aligning with a daily intention, being mindful with words and actions, is all about self-responsibility. If you want to have the life you know you desire, then you have to do something about it.

Your own vibration will not be cleared, healed or lightened up unless you choose it to be and then follow through. Wishing will not achieve anything besides some entertainment for your mind. Each day is a journey of choice, responsibility, intention and engagement.

Focus on what you want, keep the positive energy alive. We often know exactly what we do not want and speak about it easily. When you are conscious of what you are saying, then shift towards speaking about what you actually want. There is clarity, intention and a landing place for things to arrive. People often complain about getting what they don't want, and that happens simply because they are focused on that. Shift your focus and watch the ease and magic of life supporting you.

Remember whatever we speak of, goes out into the field of grace, or consciousness we are all a part of. Why not make the pathway towards what you truly want in life to be direct. If you are someone who still gets stuck in, 'I don't know what I want', then this is a perfect starting point.

Look at the things you do know, how did you get there? It is about making a decision and following through, if something does not feel right or aligned, then make another decision. Spend time with you, listen to the inner world of what you want for YOU in life and start with little decisions each day. Build your confidence towards knowing what you want.

Explore life, each moment from an open mind,
from a curiosity of what else is available or possible.

We spend so much of life unconsciously doing things, unaware and not really present, often taking things in without question. Open your mind—step outside of what you know, ask questions, see how you feel and find what really resonates.

What if something else aligns more with you? Be receptive to new ideas, new ways and new experiences. If you don't like something, tune in and see what it is that you don't like…a feeling, a sense of not enough in self, an old belief from times in the past, maybe even something your family conditioning instilled in you. With an open, curious mind you grow, expand and understand.

DECLARATION

Today, I align with my highest vibrational self and
I courageously open my heart and soul to the
expansiveness of the unknown.

ACTIVITY

Intention:

Be the best aspect of you.

Action:

- Find some space for yourself
- Close your eyes, you are instantly within
- Hand on your heart, takes your focus straight to your heart
- Then just breathe
- Feel
- Be still
- Then say, 'What am I grateful for right now?'
- Open your eyes and verbalise what is around you
- Take a deep breath and welcome the new and unknown into your awareness
- Exhale your commitment to being the best aspect of you
- Repeat this action as many times a day as you want

THANK YOU...

GRATITUDE IS AN energy I live with constantly.

No matter what shows up, I am in a portal of deep gratitude, which I offer without censor. There are so many I would like to thank, however right now, it is YOU the reader of this collection, who I bow in a gesture of Namaste.

Awareness brings healing, awakening, connection, choices and change. Life is change, no two days are the same; no two breaths are the same.

I sincerely, with all of my heart and soul, wish you deep awareness of your uniqueness, your courage, your soul and to live that with each breath, and every heartbeat.

For this book:

Stella Doyle...you are a legend! You know why and I am eternally grateful.

Gratitude for all those people who thought I could, and those who thought I couldn't.

Rachael Bermingham for really 'getting me' and telling me years ago, I had already written my books. The generosity of your input, belief, trust and friendship has inspired me to make you proud!

To my darling tribe heart and soul sistas, who totally understand me, are consistently encouraging and now and again slapping me back into reality.

Each person who has read any of my Facebook posts, articles in magazines or audiences I have presented to, each one of you is a flame that has contributed to my fire, which is part of the bigger force of evolutionary change.

BIOGRAPHY

RAELENE BYRNE, INTERNATIONALLY recognised energy transmission and activator healer, inspiring speaker, retreat facilitator and leader, meditation teacher, educator of self-empowerment through self-knowledge, writer, shamanic practitioner, Advanced liquid crystal practitioner, workshop facilitator, crystal grid creator and Earth guardian.

With decades of remembering, learning and practising, the one thing that has been a constant in Raelene's life is the power of Freewill, the expansiveness of stepping into your own unique potential and the ultimate freedom of being exactly who you ALWAYS are in any moment.

Having studied numerous forms of energetic healing, vibrational modalities, many forms of bodywork, spent years in service and support to many Hay House authors and leaders, Raelene has realised that the teachings from ancient times, that we all have everything we need within us, is indeed true. Stop, listen and act on your own inner guidance.

Raelene speaks to large audiences with an inspiring simplicity that allows each participant the gift of knowing they can be and achieve what they are truly here on Earth for.

With a treasure chest of fast, effective processes, meditations and rituals, Raelene offers the certainty for people to realise they are their own alchemists, so change becomes a dance of potential, fuelled by endless possibility.

This is as simple as saying YES to your soul's purpose.

BIBLIOGRAPHY...

Bennett, M. and Lengacher, C. (2006). Humor and Laughter may Influence Health. I. History and Background. *Evidence-Based Complementary and Alternative Medicine*, 3(1), pp.61-63.

Gilbert, E. (2016). *Brisbane Writers Festival*, Brisbane, February 2016

McGraw, P. (2001). *Self Matters / M.* New York: Simon & Schuster Source.

How Raelene can help you further...

For more information on how Raelene can guide and support you, please contact her on the following:

Website: www.raelenebyrne.com

Email: admin@raelenebyrne.com